AF580139

*Praise for*

***Happy Mother's Daze***

"A huge and charming accomplishment sure to raise the spirits of so many harried parents. Honest, fun, and wise."

—Anne Lamott, author of *Bird by Bird*

"This is a serendipitous peek into the inner world of mother and author Liz Krakow's struggles with how to give her personal best to her children in the face of life's challenges, big and small. Whether you are a parent or not, you will laugh and cry as this mother labors to ensure her children will grow up to be their personal best."

—Dr. Melba Beals, civil rights icon, member of the Little Rock Nine, author of *Warriors Don't Cry*

"Elizabeth Krakow weaves together the beautiful chaos of motherhood, marriages, and the magic of rescue dogs. A memoir that will resonate with mothers at every stage—a celebration of raising children (and husbands) with heart, humor, and hope."

—Andrea Alban, author of *Mother's Nature* and *The Happiness Tree*

"There is nothing on earth more powerful and healing than laughter, except for love, and my dear friend Liz provides them both in spades. As with everything Liz touches, this book is heartfelt and true, told with an equal measure of humility, aplomb, humor, and wonder at the miracle of life itself."

—Heather Sandy Hebert, author of *At Home in the Wine Country* and *California Coastal*

"This book is food for a hungry heart, helping us feel how much we really do matter to others. Funny, honest, and inspiring, Liz Krakow's magical, sweet writing lifted my spirits and will lift yours as well."

—Rick Hanson, PhD, author of *Buddha's Brain*, *Hardwiring Happiness*, and *Resilient*

"Profoundly moving, this book captures the poignant and hilarious moments that make parenting the best (and most frustrating) job on the planet. Such a perfect gift for new mothers!"

—Pat Ravasio, author of *The Girl from Spaceship Earth*

"This book will make you smile, laugh, and think. It ultimately serves as a reminder that motherhood is hard work, filled with grace and unexpected miracles. Truthful and compelling, it is a gift for every mother and child seeking reassurance that they are not alone in their fears, struggles, triumphs, and joys, telling the story of a fantastic family through the perspective of a strong mother, a joyful wife, and a loving daughter. Happy Mother's Day!"

—Floyd Thompkins, pastor, author of *Nobody Told Me the Road Would Be Easy*

# Happy Mother's Daze

## Confessions of Someone Flailing at Life and Parenthood

Elizabeth Krakow

**www.mascotbooks.com**

***Happy Mother's Daze: Confessions of Someone Flailing at Life and Parenthood***

©2026 Elizabeth Krakow. All Rights Reserved. No part of this publication may be reproduced, stored in a retrieval system or transmitted in any form by any means electronic, mechanical, or photocopying, recording or otherwise without the permission of the author.

The author has tried to recreate events, locales, and conversations from their memories of them. In order to maintain their anonymity in some instances, the author has changed the names of individuals and places, and may have changed some identifying characteristics and details such as physical properties, occupations, and places of residence.

**For more information, please contact:**
Mascot Books, an imprint of Amplify Publishing Group
620 Herndon Parkway, Suite 220
Herndon, VA 20170
info@mascotbooks.com

Library of Congress Control Number: 2025927687
CPSIA Code: PRV0126A
ISBN-13: 979-8-90026-005-1

Printed in the United States

*This book is dedicated to Roger, my one true love; my children, Rog III and Lucy, who raised me into motherhood; and everyone I am lucky enough to get to love.*

*May today there be peace within. May you trust God that you are exactly where you are meant to be. May you not forget the infinite possibilities that are born of faith. May you use those gifts that you have received, and pass on the love that has been given to you. May you be content knowing you are a child of God. Let this presence settle into your bones, and allow your soul the freedom to sing, dance, praise and love. It is there for each and every one of us.*

—Prayer of Saint Theresa

# Contents

# Prologue

*There are only two ways to live your life: one as if nothing is a miracle and one as if everything is a miracle.*
—Albert Einstein

One night when I was twenty-three, I slipped and fell on a ski slope outside of Boulder, Colorado, bouncing all the way down the mountain on a sheet of ice, breaking my back. I thought I was a goner. It took Mom two days to get to my bedside and it seemed like an eternity. I just needed her there—it was such a scary, uncertain time. I would need to be bathed and fed and humored for nearly three months . . . a second infancy, really. Who else but a mother would do that twice?

I remember the first question she asked my doctor when she finally stormed into my hospital room—"Will she be able to have children?" I was *mortified*. How many times had I told her I was *never* going to get married, let alone have babies?

My mother has been gone more than forty years now, and I am way older than she ever got to be. I can still hear her voice rattling around in my head as if it was yesterday. She died suddenly, of a massive heart attack, while moving my baby brother into his college dorm, leaving me with the strong impression that motherhood is actually deadly, and I clearly should avoid it like the plague.

## Prologue

I am one of those people who passionately believes everything that I think.

But dead people can be so intense and smart and persistent. It seemed my mom was everywhere once she was no longer confined to a physical body. I am absolutely haunted by her. How else can I explain my complete change of heart?

Bravely soldiering on, it was becoming increasingly obvious that the only thing that would heal the nagging, clinging, lonely void of grief would be to have a family of my own. I had been living with my sister and we were both changing jobs every six to nine months, just faking it, in that great confused fog that comes with sudden loss. We were both restless and spacey and most certainly undatable. Then this really great, funny, creative, kind guy moved in next door. He was exactly the kind of man my mom would have hand-picked, tied up with a bow, and given my phone number without asking me. My sister and I both loved him immediately. Fortunately, she got a job as a flight attendant and was traveling all the time, therefore not geographically desirable enough to really compete with me for his affection.

Alas, Roger didn't get the memo on the great romantic plans I had in store for him. He had the audacity to invite me over to see his new digs and gesture grandly: "See all this, Liz? This is a shrine to my independence." As luck would have it, he had been squandering all his romantic *notions* on the wrong gal for the past three years and when they finally broke up, he naively thought he could catch his breath and be a bachelor for a while. I remember fixating on the antique elk head he had hanging over his fireplace and thinking, "Wow: my initials are ELK! Maybe it's a sign." So, there I was—in love all by myself. Our courtship was nothing like my hopeless romantic heart had pictured. But I will always be proud of the deep knowing that I somehow had, that this was my one true love, and that gave me all the confidence I needed to be a total fool for love and risk everything to go get it. I would invite him out to the theater with friends, and he would think that I was a terrific neighbor. Sure, it was awkward, going home to the same front door, but awkward is my middle name.

After months of persistence, and many contrived moments that today might be considered stalking, he finally was able to glean the factoid that I wanted to be *more* than his extra-friendly next-door neighbor, and it was ON . . . almost as if it was really meant to be.

I loved his family right away. He was one of four hilarious brothers who were really close, and his parents were still hot for each other after thirty-five-plus years of wedded bliss. For unknown reasons, his mom liked me right away, and for those of you who understand the dynamics of reverse psychology, this caused Roger to regard me with extreme caution. After a couple years of dating, his mother invited me out to the garden after dinner one night. Like a lamb to the slaughter, I followed her, and suddenly she turned and said with great dramatic flourish, "I want to apologize for that crappy son of mine. I do *not* know why he hasn't proposed yet! You know, dear, there is only one thing to do. You simply must cut him off in the boudoir!"

Now, I am sure this was well-intentioned advice, but it was not the 1950s anymore, and I am pretty private about the olde boudoir and did not relish the thought of talking about such things with a man's mother. Before going back inside, she grabbed my arm and conspiratorially whispered, "Let's keep this conversation our little secret, dear."

I do not know what I said or how I got back in the house, but apparently most of the blood had drained out of my face. My true love took one look at my deathly pallor, then hopped up and said, "Well, I guess we better get going . . ." He gathered me into the car and then asked, "What happened to you out there?" Keeping secrets is not one of the strengths of my so-called character, so I said, robotically: "Your mom thinks I need to cut you off in the boudoir."

We overcame that little speed bump and were engaged a few months later, ushering in the roller-coaster ride of family life. I began to experience what I call "motherhood-induced Alzheimer's" setting in that first year following the birth of our adorable son Roger III, so I started writing things down to help me make sense of all the chaos and try to preserve some of the perfect little wacky moments.

Our incompetence as parents was legendary. Slippery toddler Roger seemed to know just how to evade me whenever the phone rang or my head was turned, and he was picked up by the police twice by the time he was three . . . not for any felonies per se, but because I had been encouraging him in potty training by telling him what a big boy he was and he figured that he had been emancipated. Since we were such successful parents, we were soon blessed with our darling daughter Lucy, and I was outnumbered, sleep deprived, and under water for the next fifteen or so years.

One Easter Sunday, we went with the kids to visit the cemetery and bring flowers to where Mom was buried. Four-year-old Lucy talked freely to her, and she and her brother decorated her headstone with a few jelly beans from their Easter baskets. I had such an ache to have Mom back to spend a little bit of life with her amazing grandchildren. Lucy gets extraordinarily charming and animated when it's bedtime, and that night as I was trying to talk her down and get her to sleep, she grabbed my hand and said, "I'm sorry your mommy died. But she's in heaven and you miss her and soon we will go get her and take the lid off her house and clean the dirt off her and I will say 'Grandma, I love you. Do you have any candy?' I really love you, Mom. Your hair is dirt-colored. My hair is not dirt-colored. And when I grow up, I will be your mom and take care of you! I love that story." Goodnight, Lucy-moon.

If you had asked me long ago about breaking my back, I would have said it was the worst thing that had ever happened to me. Now, with the twenty-twenty vision of hindsight, I count that accident as one of God's most tender gifts to me. It gave me three months of my mom's undivided attention in the last months of her precious life. And she got the last laugh, as I ate my words that I was never going to get married or have children.  I never did find that world-changing career that I dreamed of. I am fond of torturing myself wondering what my purpose in this life was supposed to be. What is the actual meaning of life? Becoming a wife and mother, however unnatural it was for me, was ultimately the best medicine and such a sure-fire recipe for learning those all-important lessons in love, which I am pretty sure *is* the entire meaning of life. Love is the only thing that lasts or matters on our deathbeds. Ideally, we can wake up to that little wisdom nugget well before we find ourselves on said deathbeds, and we can dare ourselves to press on to a master's degree and then maybe even a PhD in the art and science of love. And then rededicate ourselves to that goal fiercely, relentlessly, every single day.

# Prologue

I have always written down my miraculous moments so that I could sleep at night, because they pestered me until I did. These pages represent a lifetime of moments that still take my breath away. May they resonate for you and encourage you to laugh at yourself . . . or maybe just at me!

# In the Beginning . . .

In the beginning, there was true love and passion and sweet romance. And it was good.

Love begat marriage. And it was good.

Marriage begat children. And they rejoiced.

Children begat a phenomenon—not unlike a hurricane—which upended their world and created a swirl of such intensity it could only be appreciated from the hurricane's eye (if you could get there) where there was peace and the opportunity to honor its awesomeness . . . and its potential for chaos. In its wake it left a family, stronger for facing down the storms, but also the lovers, now reduced to two carcasses, who hurled themselves gratefully to bed each night, perhaps to cuddle and whisper tenderly, "You know, if I felt alive right now, I might want to try to make love."

"Thanks, Sweetie. Me too. It's the thought that counts."

And God said, "*Enough*!"

It was January 2003, and I was filled with hope that perhaps in that fresh New Year, I could reinvent myself and get it right for once. My circuits were constantly on overload, and my brain was full of a fog that I believed might be motherhood-induced Alzheimer's. I was terrified that all the precious memories that had made up my life so far would get tossed up there in that dusty attic that once housed my brain . . . just like all those photographs I'm always tossing into shoeboxes. One morning as I was having my coffee and catching up on yesterday's mail, I opened a touching personal letter from the National Alzheimer's Association, thanking me politely for my recent donation and asking me if I might actually sign my enclosed check and return it in this nice stamped, self-addressed return envelope. Try, try again. I have a picture in my mind of the letter's author grumbling to herself as she had to type this response to my small check, "Just keep the dang check, lady. You obviously need it more than we do."

When I was little, my mom loved to laugh at Erma Bombeck's and Peg Bracken's books on motherhood, and I remember telling her that she was way funnier than they were, and she should be the one writing books. I wish she had. There is so much I wish I knew about her that I never got to ask. That was the year my nine-year-old daughter was saying she wanted to be a writer (just ask "Gorge" Bush about her antiwar letter-writing campaign!), and something was spurring me to try to keep up with her.

As I reflect on those years of being a mother, I can see a string of literal and figurative heart attacks, punctuated with fleeting moments of great joy. Heart attacks are not fun for anyone, but for me it will always be the thing that got my own mother, who died way too young at forty-eight as she was moving her last born into his college dorm. So you can clearly see that motherhood not only wreaks havoc on your brain, but it can also be deadly. No one tells you how hard it really is . . . until I discovered Anne Lamott's writing. I love how she described being a mom as a strange condition where we have to watch our hearts marching around in the world completely unprotected by a rib cage and flesh, and we are supposed to somehow find a way to get comfortable with that bizarre concept. She also said that motherhood is the realization that your worst fear that something horrible might happen to your own self is now replaced by an even greater threat: that something horrible might happen to your child, and sometimes that notion can make you want to curl up in the fetal position and stay in bed. Clearly motherhood is not for the fainthearted, and I think it is safe to say it was not natural for me.

Dear Gorge,
I'm 9years old. When I grow up I want to be the first girl presedint. I'm pretty smart and I think I would be able to change the world. I know you want war but I can't help thinking about people just like me (exept alitte mores unfortunte) dyeing. Theyre as innocent as we are. It was just acouple stupid heads who blew up twin towers. Please give em a chance. I know I won't get hurt or ever hear anything but I saw pearl harbor and other war movies and I askdmy mom if thats what really happens durring the war and I just cant help it when she says yes. I hope you can find some good in you and all the stupid heads in the earth will learn to be good. could you please give me some information if it is too personal tell me.

Religon: ____________________

do you really want war?: ____________________

do you think you can make the wold a better place by war?: __________ Please send me back a hand written honest letter

Fingers crossed
Lucy G. Krakow
Peace

At least once a year, I would check in with my doctor and throw myself on the table in a clump begging him to diagnose more specifically the reason for my overwhelming exhaustion. He would look at me like I was a lunatic and/or a hypochondriac and usually suggested Valium, Prozac, exercise, and/or therapy. But there was never enough time or money for these Band-Aids, and I honestly didn't think I was depressed . . . just trying to stay alive and prevent my children from their multiple daily flirtations with death. I had to find a more creative remedy.

Alas, creativity and generally any useful electrical current to the brainal region is the first to go when one becomes a mother. My friend Robin said, "One sperm got me pregnant; the rest of them attacked all my brain cells." My theory is that a complete inability to achieve a decent night's sleep over a period of five to ten years effectively lobotomizes us to keep us on the straight and narrow path of motherhood. I was known to mumble under my breath that I was losing my marbles until once my son reminded me that I did not even have any marbles to lose. All the marbles are his—which is true.

On the physical side, for me at least, gravity and two eleven-pound C-section babies had ravaged any vanity I might have had. One last homage to Anne Lamott: "I lay down and my stomach curled up beside me." That combined with my constant daily struggle to achieve minimal daily hygiene standards such as showering, brushing my teeth, and raking my hair . . . it did not paint a pretty picture.

That word *paint* triggered a memory in the recesses of my brain: the image of my mother painting a beautiful oil portrait of each of her young children within the first five years of their lives. Now that I think about it, she never quite completed the portrait of my brother, the baby of our family. That one was different from the others . . . more painterly, ethereal, a sketch really . . . the foggier image emblematic of a harried mother's blurred focus, her standard of perfection dimmed to only the essentials. Motherhood had begun to chip away at her creativity—that life force within all of us, inspired by our Creator, which feeds our souls and makes us unique and dares us to live life with gusto and passion and imagination. I see it so naturally and universally in children;

why does that quality survive in so precious few into adulthood?

I love the story about the two-year-old who begged her parents to be left alone with the new baby for a minute, but the parents were reluctant to trust her based on the notion the average two-year-old would try to poke the new baby's eyes out at the first available opportunity. The parents ultimately agreed to allow the persistent child to be alone for a few minutes with the baby, waiting just outside the door armed with a baby monitor to listen in, just in case. All the child wanted to do was lean over the crib and ask the baby: "Tell me about God . . . I'm starting to forget."

That story spoke to my own increasing inability to focus on what I intellectually already knew was the true meaning of life: to know and love God, and my family and my fellow man, and maybe even myself if there is anything left over, with all my mind, and all my heart, and all my strength. Therein lay the conundrum—I couldn't seem to locate much strength in all this chaos.

We went to see my absolute favorite play in the world, *Les Misérables*, in San Francisco. It was the second time I'd seen it, but we had to go again to see our friend's nine-year-old son playing the role of Gavroche, the little street urchin who dies atop the rebel barricades. I knew all the lyrics and was guaranteed to cry buckets throughout, and it was all good, cheap therapy. There was a very special moment when I found myself singing along rather loudly and passionately to the lyrics "I had a dream my life would be . . . so different from this hell I'm living," and I caught my husband looking at me with absolute terror in his eyes. Fortunately, miraculously, he seemed to understand and even appreciate the perverse windmills of my mind. And I absolutely adore the refrain that came later in another song: "To love another person is to see the face of God."

# Tiaras Were Everywhere

The rhythm of parenting two young children with very different personalities was much like tap-dancing as fast as you could with a full goldfish bowl duct-taped to your midsection, while juggling six or eight ripe tomatoes at a fairly constant pace for at least eighteen out of every twenty-four hours. Repeat relentlessly seven days each week. Got it? You should also note that if you took a vacation with the family to try and escape the exhaustion of your regular routine, you needed to plan for the vacation to be as much as three times more exhausting than staying home. No one talks about this stuff.

The survival of humanity depends on us going into parenthood with our eyes wide shut. On a good day the rhythm of the tap-dancing and the juggling was in sync, effectively numbing the brain, and you made it through the day. On a bad day, you have already dropped two or three of the overripe tomatoes on your head by 8:40 a.m., and you found yourself driving your tardy six-year-old son (not a morning person) to school in your pajamas and a trench coat with fresh tomato goo dripping down your hair. On one such day, I overheard my three-year-old daughter (the princess) sigh wistfully in the back seat: "I wish sometimes there was a mother with pretty hair."

Lucy was very much a morning person. She wouldn't be caught dead leaving the house without a pretty dress, at least one tutu, and a purse carefully filled with vital plastic stuff. Although, she was usually sporting mismatched shoes on the wrong feet (sandals if it was raining, rain boots if it was sunny). Her hair was her pride and joy. She favored the "unicorn ponytail," gathering her bangs into a hair band that poked out the front of her forehead, accessorized by a dozen or so plastic clips scattered randomly throughout her matted blond hair (I was not allowed to brush it, only Daddy). She would top all that off with a tiara or a headband. I had reason to believe I was abducted by aliens and impregnated as some kind of a kinky cosmic joke. She was a marvel to behold, a real piece of work . . . and she loved to be in charge. Life with Lu never knew a dull moment.

One day when Lucy was about four, I sat with her looking through our wedding album. I noticed her frowning and asked her why.

"Why didn't you invite me to your wedding, Mom?" she asked. No amount of explaining the timeline could convince her that she hadn't been slighted. She went on to express her concern that my wedding dress really wasn't very sparkly . . . which was true. I didn't bother trying to explain to her that I had very intentionally had a dress made of a simple, crisp silk shantung, with no beading, lace, pearls, or sparkles of any kind. It was the late '80s, and thanks to Princess Diana, the princess bride look was really in. Perhaps I should have gone for it so my daughter could have respected me more. She looked pityingly up at me and suggested that perhaps we ought to have another wedding so that she could attend and then could help me pick out a really pretty dress.

It was almost our tenth anniversary, and we were long overdue for a party, so I decided to hire her as our official tenth-anniversary party planner. Invitations went out to our neighbors and most of the original wedding attendees, in a formal script that read:

*Lucy and Roger Krakow*
*Request the Honour of Your Presence*
*at*
*The Tenth Wedding Anniversary*
*of Their Parents*
*Roger and Elizabeth*
*Saturday, June 11, 1998*
*Two O'clock in the Afternoon*
*in Celebration of*
*The Ten Longest Years of*
*Their Parents' Lives*

*Bad Formal Attire Preferred*

Our trip to the fabric store for my gown was the best. We purchased yards and yards of sparkly tulle and gathered it into a skirt that made me look as big as a house. I wore the white sequin shell my mom had knitted herself for those sassy '50s cocktail parties. Lucy teased my hair into the largest mound I have ever seen, and for that special "something borrowed," we topped it all off with one of Lu's tiaras and a white feather boa. In the front yard, we erected a cheesy gazebo, festooned with fake flowers, garlands, and white "Just Married" helium balloons. Lucy walked me down the aisle, looking every inch the harried wedding planner, in one of my old satin slips and her mop of unkempt hair. My true love met me at the gazebo, adorned in a fetching lavender ruffled tuxedo shirt and a black-and-white tuxedo dinner jacket, sort of a flocked wallpaper print, looking every inch the Las Vegas lounge singer. Having just shaved off a full beard, he was now sporting large, newly carved muttonchop sideburns. He took my breath away in quite a different way than he did ten years ago . . . I still remember the strange, slightly terrifying feeling in the pit of my stomach when I looked out the window of the Santa Barbara Music Academy where we were married and saw him walking up the driveway for the rehearsal. I hadn't seen him for more than a week, and he looked so wonderful to me that I almost felt shy, or at least incredulous that that gorgeous guy was really going to marry *me*! Ah, romance . . .

But back to life in the sexy suburbs: Roger presented me with a gigantic plastic sapphire ring from a gumball machine, and the celebration really took off from there. We set up a fantastic garage band, led by my darling friend Rosa Thomas, who has one of the most soulful voices I've ever heard, and we all danced like maniacs in the driveway and out into the street. One of Roger's clients got the last laugh. Jeannine Yeomans wrote a weekly column, "North of the Gate," for the *San Francisco Chronicle*, on notable events happening in Marin. That week we made the headline: "Anniversary Bash Makes the Best of Bad Taste."

> Liz and Roger Krakow invited several hundred friends and family to the Krakow estate (their modest tract house in Corte Madera) to celebrate their tenth anniversary, bad formal attire preferred. Luckily, dozens of friends kept their ugliest bridesmaid dresses. Film producer Jennifer Thomas wore a purple bridesmaid gown, flecked with gold. Tiaras were everywhere.
>
> Neighbors Christine and Rich Walcoff (he's a KGO sportscaster) took a taxi from their house a few doors away and arrived

at the party dressed as the "cousins from hell," sporting blacked-out teeth, suitcases and hampers full of clothes for a long stay, zippers unzipped, and their children's faces smeared with peanut butter.

Can the Krakow marriage be saved? With their sense of humor, friends predict a long run.

Lucy seemed pleased with her production, and the pictures were priceless. We were blown away by close friends who flew in for our tacky gala from as far away as Texas (Roger's best man, Peter, and his wife, Tregae) and from Seattle (my love broker/bridesmaid, Anne, who had single-handedly done the most spectacular job on the flowers, including bouquets, for our original wedding). Looking back to our first wedding day, I can admit to being still overwhelmed and incredulous at the way my girlfriends and my mom's girlfriends circled their wagons and made that perfect day for us. Joani, who had been my roller-skating buddy since we were five years old, put together the most amazing food. My junior high school pal Sharon helped her, and they worked their tails off when they both deserved to be guests dancing and giggling. Special thanks to bridesmaid Terilynn's skill flirting with the lead singer in this fantastic club band one night in a bar, we got the most incredible nine-piece soul/funk dance band that we never would have been able to afford otherwise. And my lifelong friend Allison—daughter of my mom's best friend, my godmother, Carol—took the most magical photographs commemorating every detail. It all just came together, almost as if it was really meant to be.

# Mer-Mom

Lucy must be one of those old souls . . . she was always giving me advice and mothering *me*. This was not what I expected from motherhood. I foolishly thought it would be my turn to impart wisdom. But I learned to listen to her, fascinated by the innate intelligence of one so young. I suspect she had direct coaching from her grandma in the heavenly realms.

I love what Alice Walker wrote in *The Same River Twice: Honoring the Difficult*:

> I think mothers and daughters are meant to give birth to each other, over and over, that is why when love and trust have not been too badly blemished or destroyed, the teaching and learning one from the other is so indelible and bittersweet. We daughters must risk losing the only love we instinctively feel we can't live without in order to be who we are, and I am convinced this sends a message to our mothers to break their own chains, though they may be anchored in prehistory and attached to their own great grandmothers' hearts.*

---

* Alice Walker, *The Same River Twice: Honoring the Difficult,* 1st ed. New York: Scribner, 1996, p. 176.

As I fumble on through this incredible patchwork quilt that makes up life, I am continually amazed by God's promise to work all things for good for those who love him. It is a promise so rock-solid, you can take it to the bank. I will never get over that ski accident that occurred in the last year of Mom's life. It felt like it took me forever to recover—it was like a second infancy, really. I needed to be fed and bathed and carted around and humored. It was humiliating, and I was a pretty cranky, tortured, self-absorbed patient most of the time, but I don't know how I would have gotten through it without her. If you had asked me then, I would have said it was the low point of my life. Now, with the twenty-twenty vision of hindsight, I count that accident as one of God's most tender gifts to me. It gave me three months of her undivided attention in the last six months of her precious life. She was full of energy and so good at making me laugh. She would lay me down in her VW van and drive me to the movies. There I would lie down in the aisle with my head propped up on a pillow at empty matinees and eat popcorn and maybe drink a smuggled beer. I think we saw Mel Gibson in *The Year of Living Dangerously* three times. I remember the recurring theme of that movie absolutely haunting me for years to come: "Why can't you learn to love?"

Mom knew how it was done. She'd haul me up to Santa Barbara to visit my sister at UCSB, and I would bake my achy back in the hot sand, and we'd salute the sunset with a margarita. She was always happiest at the beach, and I always picture her there. I absolutely treasured that time together, although I know it must have strained her heart. God knows my own heart so well, and how impossible and unprocessable it would have been for me to have had to have her just leave us so suddenly without getting to say goodbye, and without having spent that chunk of time with her. But I often tell people that when you lose someone you love, you can sometimes feel their love more intensely once it is no longer encumbered by a physical body. You can wear their love in a pocket close to your heart where it is always handy, and it is positively there for you whenever you need it. And I know for sure Mer-Mom, my pet name for her, is pleased to know that my ski accident did in no way hamper my ability to have children—at least not physically anyway.

*Slowly I find myself being weaned from her material presence. Yet filled with her as never before. It is I now who represent us both. I am our mutual past. I am my mother and my self. She gave me love, to love myself, and to love the world. I must remember how to love.*

—Toby Talbot, *A Book About My Mother**

My poor mother . . . my adolescent years were predictably dicey, but not in the predictable ways. Mom was such a free spirit that my rebellion of choice was to be a really good student and a well-behaved dullard fond of babysitting, watching TV, or reading books on Friday and Saturday nights. It was truly cruel, passive-aggressive behavior on my part designed to totally drive her crazy. On one such night, I remember her losing it completely, and she yelled, "Why don't you go out and smoke some marijuana or drink some beer like a normal kid?"

Slowly I began to branch out, and she was so relieved that she allowed me a ton of latitude and freedom. But dates with actual boys were a rarity. On my sixteenth birthday, a dozen long-stemmed yellow roses arrived with a greeting card signed, "Happy Birthday, love, Mr. E." Get it? Mystery! I never found out who did that . . . it was probably a mercy offering from my parents. I'm sure they meant well, but then I went on to make a total fool of myself asking cute boys that I hoped had sent them if they had sent them, and no one would cop to it. I had a serious crush on the boy next door, who was cute and smart and actually taller than I was, which was a *huge* aphrodisiac at the time, but he was way out of my league. He used to come over and watch *Fernwood 2 Night* and *Saturday Night Live* sometimes, since I could usually be found at home if I wasn't babysitting. One night I so clearly remember feeling his eyes on me and I dared myself to meet them, and he gave me my first really passionate kiss, and it stirred my hormones up something fierce. It was all I could think about for a long time. Unfortunately, he was also doing that with several of my close girlfriends, as well as older, popular beauty queens, whose comings and goings I could easily

* Toby Talbot, *A Book About My Mother*, 1st ed. Farrar, Straus, & Giroux, 1980, p. 111.

witness from my stalking perch in the upstairs windows of our house.

I was the coeditor of the school yearbook in my senior year, and one day when I was alone in the yearbook office working on a deadline, he came in with a funny look on his face, dropped an envelope on my desk, and left immediately. I opened it, and inside it read, "Congratulations. You have been nominated for the Homecoming Court." Normally this might be an occasion for happiness, but I swear, I had just seen the movie *Carrie*, and all I could think was that I was going to be the laughingstock of the entire school, and that this was meant only to mock and humiliate me publicly. Which, of course proved true when Marion Mapes and Sue Buck were elected. I had such a pathetic inability to experience joy or other positive emotions.

Around this time, I discovered the magical ability of music to elevate my oppressive moodiness. There was a group of funny, smart, and geeky guys that year who formed a band to tour the neighborhoods on Friday and Saturday nights to stave off boredom. They called themselves the Mele Kalikimaka Good-Time Band, and our house was their most appreciative audience. They were spectacularly untalented musically, but also really creative and frustrated and brilliantly gifted at dork fun. One of their dads had a flatbed truck, and that became their mobile stage. It was soon apparent that what they needed was a bad girl singer to tour with them, and I got the nod. I grabbed a tambourine, put on a green polyester knit dress and a red crushed velvet hat that made me look like a cross between the Church Lady and the Flying Nun, and off we went to spread our discordant message. It gave Mom a lot of hope that all was not lost for me, and it got us through the desert of that last year before I left home for college.

Mom was so worried that I was completely emotionally lame, which of course I was. It was a little too late to remedy this sad fact since I was essentially born that way, but no one had really noticed until my tortured teen years. I remember Mom really trying to tutor my sister and me in the art of flirting since we were both pretty hapless socially. We would pull into the gas stations in the old days, when there was always some clean-cut guy who would greet you and ask if he could check under your hood, and Mom often would remark that he was being exceptionally polite, probably because of us girls, and remind us that we should really go for a guy like that who could fix things.

"I'm so sure, Mom," we would huff, rolling our eyes.

One of my favorite memories involves driving home one day from high school with my sister Meredith, who had been elected sophomore princess on the Homecoming Court. The big issue of the day was that the homecoming dance and coronation were the next night, and she still didn't have a date. I wasn't much help in that area, but then we were driving home and passed this guy walking down the street that we recognized from the water polo team who went to a different school. It seemed like a godsend. We pulled over and offered him a ride, and by the time we dropped him off at home, she had casually mentioned that there was a dance at school the next night asked if he would like to come. He said, "Sure!" He showed up the next night wearing jeans and this funny ultrasuede jacket that was trendy in the '70s, and was he ever surprised to find he was escorting one of the homecoming princesses, in her sparkling Quiana gown!

About a year before Mom died, we were all home for a summer visit, having dinner at our favorite dive fish-and-chips place in the marina near our house. The whole family including Grandma and Grandpa were there, when two darling surfed-out guys walked past our noisy group and said hello as they passed us with their takeout orders heading to their beautiful sailboat tied up on the nearby dock. A moment later, they returned and struck up a conversation with Mom, who loved a good flirt. It turned out that they had actually built this gorgeous wooden boat themselves. They apologized for their scruffiness, saying they would love to invite my sister and me to join them for a tour. As much as we would have loved to torture Mom by declining their offer, we just couldn't do it this time. We hopped up and followed them down to their boat, which had been lovingly handcrafted to look like a classic old schooner. It had a woodburning fireplace in a corner and inlaid cabinetry that was not to be believed. We popped open some beers and settled into a completely natural conversation that lasted long enough to worry our parents and grandparents, who eventually ventured on down the gangplank to check on us.

Grammy and Gramps were especially entranced, because their oldest son, my uncle Don, had built his own twenty-five-foot sailboat and traveled around the world when he was about their age. The sun was setting, and it was time to go, but we weren't ready for it to end, so we told Mom and Dad that our new friends had offered to sail us home. They agreed, and off we sailed on a hot summer night with two total strangers we had just met. We sailed past a wedding reception on an outdoor deck, and we threw down the anchor right there and danced on the deck and howled at the moon until after midnight.

I don't know why I am telling this story, except that it was sort of a perfect moment, and it paints such a picture in my mind. Our actions that night may have been intended as a stealth revenge on Mom, sort of calling her bluff for always harping on us to flirt and live it up a little and showing off that we were fully capable of doing it if we wanted to. For once, Mom had the joy of checking her watch for a few hours and worrying that we might actually have been abducted by pirates. We all became great friends with Gary and Richard, and they ended up moving that gorgeous boat to the empty dock behind our family's house to stay for a few years. The day after we all met, my sister went back to college, and I went back to work in Colorado, so the romance factor never quite got to blossom. Years later though, on the day I finally got married, Richard met and fell in love with my sister's best friend, Dawn, and they were married two years later . . . so there was a kind of circuitous magic in that evening, even though the romance wasn't meant for us.

# A Healthy Baby Boy . . .

*And the father is recovering nicely.*

I'd gone in for a routine exam during the last week of my first pregnancy. I was so large, I was stopping traffic wherever I went, so they decided to do some quick calculations on the baby's size to make sure I wasn't having quadruplets. They estimated that the baby was already at least eleven pounds, and under the circumstances, they offered me an elective C-section. Apparently delivering a baby that size could bring on a host of cringeworthy physical atrocities, which I prefer not to revisit. I had not even read any of the chapters in my pregnancy books on C-sections, thinking that with my large childbearing hips, it wasn't even an option. But in my heart of hearts, I had to admit that I had always kind of thought it sounded like a great way to go . . . fifteen minutes and you have your baby, versus fifteen-plus hours of primal screaming . . . and let's face it, where would *you* rather have stitches?

Be careful what you wish for. I told them that if they would do it right now, I'd go for it to avoid the prospect of going home and freaking out. I checked right into the hospital, and they planned the surgery for first thing in the morning.

First thing in the morning turned out to be 5:30 a.m. after a sleepless night of listening to the woman in the next bed pant and moan all night. My husband was a little foggy after trying to doze on a little cot next to me and having been served quite a few beers late that night at the corner pub celebrating the coming blessed event with his brother Chad.

The nurse drove the IV forcefully into the top of my hand and trundled me into the iceberg-cold operating room before I could protest. It all began to happen so fast. Eight or ten people swarmed around me, telling me that I would feel some pulling and tugging, and then baby would be out. They stationed the anesthesiologist and my husband on either side of my head behind the drape, which kept us from seeing any gore. Suddenly, I felt burning and stinging, and I turned to the anesthesiologist to alert him, and he got immediately defensive and yelled at me: "The baby will be out in five minutes . . . can you take it?"

"I don't know," I said. "This is creeping me out!"

"Well, if you can't take it, I'm going to have to put you out," he admonished me.

"But I don't want to miss my first baby being born! You're the doctor! Can't you just give me more juice so I'm not partially numb?" I screeched hysterically.

The macho jerk slapped a mask over my mouth to shut me up, and I thought it must mean I'd soon be going under, but instead the nicest thing happened: I sort of levitated out of my body on nitrous oxide and watched the whole scene from somewhere near the ceiling. In the meantime, I noticed my darling husband was conspicuously absent. No one wanted to alarm me at the time, but as I was arguing with the jerky anesthesiologist, Roger was empathizing very strongly with me, imagining just how super it would feel having your guts hanging out on the table without anesthesia, and he began to swoon. Apparently, he felt it coming, let go of my hand, and attempted to crab walk out of the icy room. My sister and in-laws were waiting just outside for the big news when they heard the cry, "We need more doctors in here, *stat*!"

Meredith said her heart just sank as she pictured something going terribly wrong with me or the baby. My mother-in-law, Sally, claimed that she instinctively knew it had something to do with her firstborn son, which was validated as two orderlies dragged her six-foot-six son out of the operating room by his ankles. They wrangled him up onto a gurney and tried to revive him, but it took longer than usual, and they were worried that he might be having a seizure, as he seemed to be flailing around trying to get back from wherever he was so he wouldn't miss our baby being born. When he finally came to, they got him some juice and rolled him into the doorway just in time for him to feebly announce: "It's Roger III! I'm there for you, Liz!"

In my laughing gas reverie, I yelled back, "But where are you?"

"Eight twelve," the doctor announced.

"What? You said the baby was at least eleven pounds!" Gurney Boy protested from across the room.

"That is the time of birth, sir," said the doctor. "The baby weighs eleven pounds, four ounces."

I was vaguely thrilled to have a baby boy and to put the whole surreal morning behind me, but the truth was I was feeling about as dingy as I ever had in my life. They rolled us both into recovery together, side by side on our his 'n' her gurneys, and they had to recruit my sister to come in and hold the baby, since we were already proving ourselves unfit for parenthood. We had the whole place to our bad selves at that crazy hour of the morning.

It took me a while before I could imagine going through all that again. I was determined to do Lucy's birth differently, just as soon as I got back from my dear friend Terilynn's wedding. I had sworn to be there unless I was actively in labor, even though it was a five-hour drive away, and my doctor and mother-in-law had specifically forbidden me to make the trip. The amazing will of Lucy to order my universe soon began asserting itself even from the womb. The Friday night before the wedding, I spent midnight to 6:00 a.m. in the bathtub with a magazine, just trying to keep my muscles from spasming. It didn't seem like I was in labor, but I couldn't ignore it, either, and I definitely couldn't sleep. About 3:30 in the morning, my husband checked in on me to see what was going on, and since I'd never once sent him out on one of those pregnancy-related pickles and bon-bon larks, I took him up on his offer to pick up some more trashy magazines to read to help me pass the time.

By 6:30 a.m. there was a definite rhythmic quality to the discomfort, and I figured it meant I wasn't going to the wedding but should check things out at the hospital. My neighbor Dee, who works at the hospital, called ahead to see who was on duty and assured me that I was in great hands, with an all-female team who had helped deliver her own babies. We called Roger's parents to meet us at the hospital to cover the big-brother-sitting duty. It is significant to say here that my mother-in-law had a real interest in the baby being born that day. Her husband was to turn seventy in exactly one week. He had specified that he didn't want a party, and she'd said, "Fine, we'll make it the baby's christening!" The invitations went out to all their friends, and we had to get a guest of honor, and fast! What do you get the guy who has it all?

We all met at the hospital early Saturday morning, and I went in for the checkup. After monitoring, they decided that I wasn't in real labor and that they would have to send me home. I was a tad cranky after being up all night, and my mother-in-law leaped to my defense: "You are not going to send her home! She is exhausted and scheduled for a C-section on Monday, and she won't make it until then. We are here now, so have a heart!"

They agreed to let me stay until noon or so, but unless things progressed, they had no choice but to send me home. After our nightmarish last delivery, I had been in the care of the head of the department of high-risk pregnancies. He had been so wonderfully reassuring that I agreed to schedule another C-section after he promised to do it himself, and he didn't work weekends. I had hoped for the natural childbirth experience, but after dieting my whole pregnancy, the longest nine months of any woman's life, the baby was still looking like a whopper, and they encouraged another Cesarean.

About this time, we heard someone out in the hall saying there was a man named Jim looking for his daughter, who was somewhere on the floor in labor. My husband and I wondered how my dad could have made the trip up here so fast. We didn't expect him to come, as he was supposed to be at the wedding five hours away. So Roger left me alone with his mother and went off looking for my lost dad. Curiously we never found that phantom man named Jim, as my dutiful dad was at the wedding where he was supposed to be.

Now, ever since Roger and I were just dating, there had been an established rule that I was not to be left alone with his mother, or bizarre things would happen. Under the intense circumstances of that moment, the rule was overlooked, with predictably chaotic consequences. As soon as Roger left the room, Sally came over to my bed and placed her hand lightly on my abdomen, and I swear, instantly triggered the tsunami-contraction-from-hell, which broke my water and made me surrender all romantic notions I may have had about natural childbirth. My mother-in-law turned white as a sheet, and sort of backed away from me and called for the nurse to come. Our petite ten-pound, eight-ounce Lucy arrived a short while later, cheerfully and stresslessly delivered by an all-female team—including an adorable anesthesiologist named Lucy, as we all chatted about the wedding we were missing at that exact moment. A week later we all made it to the christening/seventieth birthday event, thanks to the miracle of Vicodin.

We liked to joke that my mother-in-law made Martha Stewart look like an amateur. Given what you already know about me, I can imagine you are thinking oil and water just don't mix. For unknown reasons, she has always liked me, and has been my champion since day one, which was sort of the kiss of death for any of you who understand the principles of reverse psychology in the parent-child relationship. For Roger, the fact that his mother approved of me caused him to approach me with extreme caution when we were dating.

Following the dreaded incident in the garden in which I was instructed to "cut him off in the boudoir," the brothers Krakow created a new house rule that it would be best if I were not left unsupervised with Roger's mother. I remember at the next family dinner, she said, "Liz, come upstairs and see what I'm going to wear to the opera opening!" Bang! All four brothers hopped chivalrously into action and said, "We want to see too, Mom!" Bless their hearts.

Since I became a mother, there have been so many idiotic moments that I have come to believe in and rely firmly on a God who stands by us and helps us in very practical ways, or my children would not have thrived as they did. Little tasks go unexpectedly haywire for the sleep-deprived mother, like the time I tried to simply drop off some dry cleaning, with a child dozing in his car seat. I grabbed an armful of clothes and accidentally caught the automatic door lock with my ample hip as I closed it. I now had a child waking up and wanting to be picked up that I couldn't get to. I knew it would take at least forty-five minutes on a good day for AAA to come bail us out. Should I leave him alone and crying and run to the pay phone on the corner or grab that tall man with the scraggly hair getting into his car over there (who looked a little like Charles Manson in hindsight) to pinch-babysit? Incredibly, I opted for the latter and nabbed a wire coat hanger from the dry cleaners to wrestle the door open. Disaster averted for the day.

We human beings like to think that we learn from our mistakes, and it gives us great comfort to believe that. I kid you not—a few months later, my sister and I were unloading groceries from our Costco run out the back of her station wagon and into mine. I dragged a crate of groceries across the tailgate door and tripped the lock of her fancy new car, and the same thing happened—this time with all the windows up tight on a day of record-breaking heat. To improve the drama this time, the engine was running in a no-parking zone with her twin babies screeching in their car seats. Needless to say, we created a commotion. The fire department arrived with their slim-jim. The babies were crying so hard, the windows were fogging up. Meredith was hysterical, begging the firemen to just break a window because one of the selling points of her new car was how theft-proof it was. Out of nowhere a man named Manuel showed up, saying he worked at the tire shop on the corner and thought he might be able to help. He was sporting a slim-jim, too, so we had little hope, but he had the car open in seconds and then disappeared before we could properly thank him. I went to the tire shop on the corner, but they didn't know of him. He was a godsend. Who was it that said, "The definition of insanity is doing the same thing over and over, expecting a different outcome?"

# Potty Training Batman

I remember reading some writing advice to "write as if everyone you know is dead." I would just amend that to "write as if I myself am dead" because it will free me up to tell the whole awful truth without fear of the Department of Social Services showing up on my doorstep to find a decent home for my children. By the time my son was three years old, the police had picked him up twice. He loved the police. Whenever things were a little dull, he seemed to know the police were good for a little adventure. One day we were helping my brother Andrew and his wife, Gwen, move into their first home. There were five adults and one small child. There was a really neat playhouse in their new backyard, and it seemed safe for me to run to the hardware store, with an excellent ratio of four adults to keep an eye on the one sweet boy. When I returned forty minutes later and asked after him, Dad, Grandpa, Aunt, and Uncle all looked at each other and said, "I thought you had him . . . he's around here somewhere . . ."

I ran around and discovered the side gate of the yard was ajar. He was gone. We fanned out into the neighborhood. There was a hideously busy street a block away. I could hardly breathe, but I got to the phone and choked out the red alert that my two-and-a-half-year-old blond boy was missing. The dispatcher immediately reassured me: "I think we have him." Moments later he rolled up to the curb in a fancy police car, blissed out in the back seat, hugging a giant police dog and holding a candy cane.

Since things were going so well with our son, my husband and I decided (incredibly!) that we were ready to welcome yet another precious bundle into the world. I was thinking that it would be wise to start potty training so we would have just the one in diapers. Potty training can be one of the great challenges in parenting, so as you can imagine, we were likely to excel at this one too. A friend recommended a video called *Once Upon a Potty* that worked magically for them. We couldn't afford cable, so the only TV we ever watched was video, and the potty movie was a huge novelty. We watched it again and again and again. We supplemented the training with real-world practice and repeated words of encouragement: "You are such a big boy now," etc.

One day, about halfway through my pregnancy with our second baby, I met a friend for lunch to discuss my recent traumatic amniocentesis. Something had been funky on one of the early screening tests, and they thought there was a chance the baby might have Down syndrome. It was all very stressful because they also asked us to sign some disclaimer that said we understood that the tests might prove the baby was fine, but in very rare cases, the amnio itself might cause the pregnancy to fail. My husband and I discussed the fact that every parent knows that there is a chance of birth defects going into a pregnancy and that we didn't really need to risk an amnio. He even said that he always kind of thought God might give him a special-needs child because God knew he could handle it. I have always treasured that comment as one of the sweetest things he has ever said. But then the doctors said that if the child had a certain kind of Down syndrome, there is a 1 in 350 chance that the baby would die within the first two weeks. I congratulated them on finally hitting on the one horror I was pretty sure I could not handle and in the nicest possible way, told them they had successfully ruined my pregnancy and that the stress of losing sleep over this for the next four and a half months would probably do more damage to my unborn child than their giant horse needle, so go ahead—have at it!

Following an amnio, they advise you to take it very easy for the next ten days to avoid a miscarriage, and I was really trying, but as the mother of a three-year-old boy with Batman fantasies, it was so clearly impossible. That fateful day as my girlfriend was attempting to talk me down out of my amnio drama tree, my boy was happily running circles around our table at the little sidewalk café while we talked. In the blink of an eye—I *swear*—he was gone. We could clearly see for a block in either direction. My girlfriend affirmed for me that *yes*! He was here just a split second ago. We asked everyone we saw to help. I felt down deep in my bones that it had to be foul play for it to have happened so suddenly and insidiously. He was the new missing child on the milk carton for sure. My emotions were over the top as I again made the dreaded 911 call. Five police cars arrived within minutes. He had been missing for nearly twenty minutes without a clue. I could barely answer their questions—he was wearing a Batman T-shirt . . . blond hair . . . blue eyes . . . comes up to about my belly button. I found myself concentrating on my Lamaze breathing skills to carry me through this unbearable pain. For variety, I tortured myself with the threat of this stress causing me to miscarry.

Forty minutes went by, and there wasn't much left of me when incredibly a police car pulled up with a small, fearless boy in the back seat. He had made his way to the nearby park where we often went after shopping. It wasn't possible, we said! We would have seen him! So he showed us the secret way through the back of the café that led to an alley and on toward the playground, about a football field away. The policeman found him by his Batman T-shirt, not missing me a bit, playing by the swings. When the policeman approached him and asked him his name he said, "Batman." Obviously. The policeman told him he was too little to go to the playground without his mommy, and he stomped his feet and said, "I'm not little! My mommy says I'm a *big* boy because I go potty on the toilet!" The nice policeman turned Batman back over to me and said, "You sure have your hands full, lady."

I was badly shaken. I turned to my old friend Amy, who had successfully raised four great children into double digits, and begged her for advice. The first thing she said was "How much coffee are you drinking?"

"Never more than a cup a day," I lied, thinking she was going to make me give it up.

"Double it," she said. "It is your only hope of cranking your energy up to their levels. Find a good church that will rev your engines every week. Also, I think it's important to drop your standards in the housecleaning department a notch."

I took her advice to heart and forged on bravely. A few years later, I had to call her to let her know I had perhaps taken her advice too far, in yet another close encounter of the police kind. We had moved into a little two-bedroom condo while we were remodeling our house for four months. It had a great pool, and it felt like a vacation. The kids would run back and forth from the pool to get snacks, goggles, etc. One day we were at the pool, and Lucy ran back for something and left the front door of the condo wide open. Fortunately, my husband came home right behind her to get something he had forgotten and closed things up . . . however, a moment later a policeman knocked on the door and asked for his identification, which of course showed the address of the house we were remodeling. He definitely had some explaining to do. The policeman told him a neighbor had called to report that our condo's door had been left standing open and that it appeared to have been ransacked. Roger sheepishly explained that we were perhaps a little challenged in the housecleaning area and that we would try harder in the future. I don't share that story with just anyone.

I'm seeing a pattern emerge here of police stories, the kind you rarely see on TV. One of my favorites happened when I finally had both kids in school, and I was starting to think I could get a life. Beware. My mother-in-law had tickets to *Giselle* at the San Francisco Opera and invited my new sister-in-law, Sheila, and me. I made the effort to secure a driving babysitter so that the kids could make their after-school activities and I could make it to the lovely restaurant Jardinière in San Francisco by 5:30. Ah, best-laid plans. Unfortunately, the sitter's car wouldn't start at the absolute last minute, so I had to try to get all the pickups covered myself. It was eighty degrees outside, and I was dressed for failure in a lovely sleeveless silk dress. My husband regularly mocks me for driving like an old lady, but I was reviewing my ridiculous schedule in my head and was apparently going sixty miles per hour in a forty-mile-per-hour zone and got pulled over. I dramatically, almost accusingly, explained to the poor policeman that my sitter's car broke down and that I had to pick up Lucy and her friend Sarah at kindergarten at 3:30, dress them in the car to make ballet at 3:45, get Roger to batting practice by 4:00, swing by my job to get the press release copy approved, loop over to grab the sitter at 4:45, scoop up Roger at batting practice at 5:00, and get all three back to the house and somehow get myself into the city at rush hour by 5:30! The policeman had every right to be offended by my tirade, but he miraculously let me off with a stern warning . . . I think I may have impressed him with my pitted-out silk dress clinging alluringly to my womanly bulges. I thanked him, flung myself back behind the wheel, threw the car into reverse, and . . . clipped his motorcycle!

I kid you not. I turned off the ignition—mind you, I was now sixteen minutes late to pick up the kindergarteners. I got out of the car, just shaking and sobbing, thrust my hands into the air and said, "Arrest me, Officer. Take me away to solitary confinement or a nice, padded cell. I cannot explain how that just happened . . ." Apparently my rubber bumper had just loudly thunked his tire, and there was no actual damage, so I didn't get to go to jail or anything that therapeutic. He could *not* have been nicer, and I really suspect he wasn't a real cop at all, but an angel from God trying to save me from myself. I still can't quite believe that one. *Slow down!*

The story ends as I arrived at the lovely restaurant, after hitting every red light between home and the opera house, incredibly only a half hour late. My mother-in-law and childless/sweat-free sister-in-law were cool and collected at a table perilously near Joe and Jennifer Montana. My mother-in-law greeted me as I schlepped up the stairs: "We don't want to hear it! We are having a perfectly lovely time."

I'm not proud of this, but I took the bait: "That's too bad because I have never had an excuse this good!"

"Well, you'll have to order first because they will need this table," she insisted.

"Fine. I will be drinking my dinner." And I ordered two martinis to come at the same time to vent my spleen, and saluted myself for another successful, full-lived day.

I especially loved sharing this moment with Joe and his stunning, completely sweat-free wife, Jennifer, because it really affirmed for me how far I had come in the ten years since I last dined with Joe. In one of my truly defining moments of haplessness as a single gal, I happened to be in the bar of Pizzeria Uno in the Marina, San Francisco, on Saint Patrick's Day. My spinster sister and I were waiting for a table with our dad and brother, who were up visiting. My brother, the sports fan, glanced across the crowded bar, and exclaimed, "OH MY GOSH! THAT'S JOE MONTANA!" My sister and I were vaguely familiar with the name since the 49ers had just won the Super Bowl, and Joe's darling face had been on the cover of *TIME* magazine. He was being swarmed for autographs, mostly by women, as he was then San Francisco's number one bachelor. It made my brother's night. He monitored the scene intently, including us in the play-by-play. At one point he said it appeared that Joe kept looking over at us. "Have another beer," we said. After about an hour, we were seated—behold!—just a few tables away from Joe and an unidentified male companion.

My brother was facing them, and he repeatedly insisted: "I swear you guys—he keeps looking over here! You have *got* to go over and get his autograph!"

"Why don't *you* go get his autograph? We do not want to be in the same club as all those squirrelly girls that have been hassling them all night. I feel sorry for them," I said, doing my little superior dance. "However, just for fun, I think I have an idea. Trust me, Mere . . . let's go."

We stood up and sauntered over to their table when there was a break in the parade of fans, feeling every bit of our several beers giving us liquid courage. I had a cocktail napkin in my hand and a pen, and I went up to Joe's dining companion and said, "You look very familiar. Are you, like, Joe Montana's friend or something?"

He laughed. "I'm Joe's cousin actually, Michael Montana."

"Great!" I said. "Could you give us your autograph so that our brother the football fanatic over there can relax?"

Joe looked confused and slightly stricken, so I tossed him the napkin and said, "Here, you can sign this, too, if you like." He did. We chatted awhile, and it seemed kind of natural when they said, "Why don't you gals sit down and join us for a beer?" At that, my elaborate self-protective-dating-sabotage instincts kicked in, and I quickly, said, "Thanks, but we really couldn't. You see over there?"—my brother waved—"We're actually here with our dad and brother, so we should probably get going. Nice to meet you!" Dash! Excellent play, gals.

My brother lost all respect for us for the rest of our lives. Mercifully, I do not believe Joe recognized me that night, a decade later at Jardinière, in all my stressed-out splendor . . . he appeared to be fully entranced by the perfectly lovely woman he had been destined to marry.

# Coco

Allow me one last highly dramatic police-story episode, and I promise I'll try to move on from all that. Sometimes when I'm driving all alone in my car, it's like being in a sensory-deprivation chamber, and the rare quiet of it all is so foreign and surreal that it can totally overstimulate my brain. No good can possibly come from this. Enough said. This is a story from my journal, several years into the marriage.

A flash flood of tears blurred my vision along about Gilroy as I was driving south on 101 at about eighty miles an hour. I was thinking about Coco again. Something about being alone on the open road made her come rushing back into my thoughts with a vengeance. She, too, had been alone in her car that November day . . . and her birthday was just last week . . . and the anniversary of the accident was coming up . . . and at that very moment, I was supposed to be at a clambake at the beach hosted by her husband and his new wife. It's always something, as Gilda Radner would say (another one of my favorite dead people).

Dead people can be so intense. I am absolutely hounded by them. I've come to believe that people who were so alive in this life become larger than life in the great beyond. Coco and I were new friends, really; our desks faced each other at work. Often, we'd drown our work-related frustrations in a couple of beers at the bar across the street, daydreaming about the next moves we needed to make in our not-so-brilliant careers. We wanted to do so many of the same things: rehab old houses, import Italian pottery, become professional matchmakers. Do you think it is possible for a friendship to bloom and grow even after death? Did she know how much I loved her? In so many subtle, clever Coco-like ways, she tells me she does . . .

Just moments ago, a cop pulled me over for driving erratically in the midst of my teary, sentimental episode. He seemed startled to find me in such an emotional state and asked me if everything was all right. "My friend Coco died," I said as I blew my nose. He said he was sorry and sent me on my way without the ticket I deserved, probably thinking I was on my way to a funeral. There was never an opportunity to confess that I was so vividly mourning a loss that had occurred almost four years ago . . . score one more for you, Coke!

When I first joined the office, I spent many idle hours gazing across the desk at her beautiful face and marveling at her forthright, confident manner. I would take notes while staring at my phone, daring it to ring. We were real estate agents, and we both had to admit that we were nowhere near being in our element there. Originally the work had appealed to me because of the attractiveness of being my own boss, earning according to what I put into it—not having to ask some foul-mouthed, sexist, tightwad, drug-abusing, spoiled-brat-whose-daddy-gave-him-the-job for a long overdue raise. Okay, so I'd been burned by corporate America and may still harbor some tiny issues with forgiveness, so help me God. I was sincerely trying to pull myself up by my own bra straps and take charge of my own destiny . . . and I hoped that it would include that amazing man I'd been dating for two years, and perhaps a funky little house with manageable mortgage payments in the not-too-distant future. So real estate was actually kind of a logical step, even if my heart never was quite in it. The workplace doesn't want your heart anyway. It just gets in the way. This time I vowed I'd be tough, professional, motivated to succeed financially, liberated by my newfound independence. I'd become one of those real estate barracudas with a late-model Mercedes, big hair and lacquered nails, and practical pumps. Dear God, this was going to be a disaster.

Coco couldn't help but notice my panic, and she took it upon herself to show me the ropes . . . often holding herself out as an example of what *not* to do. Her frankness often got her into trouble in a business where ass-kissing paid real dividends. We were residential leasing agents, a training ground for sales at our firm. We were essentially a public relations entity responsible for keeping properties happily leased until the time came to sell, and then they would come to our company as listings, uncontested, in the perfect world. We were privileged to work with a lot of spoiled, wealthy landlords who were only too happy to pay our commissions when we brought them squeaky clean tenants with too much cash in the bank, who absolutely adored cheap brown paneled walls, shag carpeting, and cottage cheese ceilings. The minute we tried to place a tenant who needed to negotiate in any way, or someone who didn't quite measure up to the tenant of their dreams . . . watch out. Coco didn't sugarcoat it whenever she smelled discrimination or anything unethical. It tanked a lot of deals for her.

One of the things we had to do each morning was go out to price new listings and look at property. Coco could be a distracted driver—coming from these lips, I'm sure you would agree that is indeed a very dangerous situation. She was always talking, gesturing, pulling over impulsively when she'd spy a parking space so we could grab coffee. She was a magnet for people and really smart about them. Everyone loved her. Her husband's best friend, Jim, was probably the president of her fan club. He was single and a little frustrated, because I think he was holding out for someone just like Coco, and that was a pretty big order. She was always setting him up with friends of hers with comic results.

It was possible to completely burn out in our business. We were expected to be in the office for normal business hours, but the reality was the greatest demand for our time from our clients was nights and weekends. I was determined to throw myself into my work, to prevent myself from obsessing on the unhappy fact that it was becoming increasingly clear that my boyfriend of two years was never going to get around to asking me to marry him, thanks to my erratic, needy, schizophrenic, overly emotional behavior over the past two-plus years. Also, I was overweight, bad at dating, and in general had a bad attitude. I'm way too high maintenance, and I lived with my roommate, Anne, who was fond of regularly taking him out on the sidewalk and yelling, "*Liz is the best thing that will ever happen to you, and you are a complete idiot for not seeing that!*" She had all the markings even then of the world-class attorney she was to become.

One Wednesday in early November 1987, I decided to take off work and do nothing to see if I could recharge my batteries. It turned out my spinster sister, Meredith, was in town on a layover, so we made plans to have lunch and maybe go to a matinee. When Rog found out we were playing hooky, he decided he, too, could take the day off. One of Roger's finest qualities, and I have no idea how this could have happened for a man raised with three brothers, is his highly evolved feminine side. I can throw him in with any arrangement of my girlfriends, and he can groove successfully. It's kind of miraculous. I know of at least two of my single girlfriends who have offered to step right up and move in and play stepmother to my children if and when I spontaneously combust. I think the world would be a better place if there were a few more like him out there. However, back in November of 1987, I was more than a little frustrated with him. And here he was, wedging himself into my great escape with my sister. Not only that, but he also conned me into spending the night on his sailboat in Sausalito that Tuesday night, effectively squeezing my sister out of the deal. She'd planned to grab a ride over the bridge with Roger's brother Chad the next day to join us for a sail. Roger popped up early Wednesday morning and said he was going to run to the store to get a picnic together, and then he sneakily called his brother and told him to make up some excuse to my sister, saying he couldn't make it, so that we could be alone. I woke up that morning, groggier than usual, because I can never really sleep on a boat—it's always rocking, lines clanking, wood expanding and contracting, moaning and groaning. Roger soon returned with provisions, and the news that unfortunately, mysteriously, and conveniently, Meredith and Chad would not be able to join us for our sailing adventure.

It was a gorgeous sunny day, and we had the whole San Francisco Bay to ourselves. I had my nose in a good book and was completely at peace in the sweats that I had slept in, and I could hardly be bothered to hop up and pull in a line or hoist the anchor as we pulled into a little cove behind Angel Island. Fortunately, Roger seemed to have a kind of hyper energy. I noticed that in between anchoring, rustling up a beautiful barbecue of shrimp and veggies, and putting on music and filling my beverage orders, he was paying great attention to his Italian studies. We had spent ten days in Italy together, just six months before, and if I ever get really brave, I'll tell you our story about Verona, city of doomed lovers, but I just cannot quite go there now. That trip had inspired Roger to learn Italian so that he could communicate with my Aunt Rosetta, who is possibly the most adorable human on the planet, and so that he could ask directions on trains, and I wouldn't always be struggling to suppress my overwhelming urge to strangle him on delightful vacations.

After a lovely lunch, I looked at my watch and said, "Oh, we've gotta go! Your mom expects us to be at your house by 3:00 for your dad's birthday dinner!"

Rog quickly said, "No. I think we've got a half hour here. Can I get you some grappa?" He poured each of us a generous portion of grappa, a varnishlike liquor that we had discovered one fateful day in Verona, when we discovered its supernatural power to steady one's nerves when one is not coping well with life organically. The grappa burned as it slid down my throat, and I focused my eyes harder to read the first newspaper I'd attempted to read all week. In the background noise, I could hear Roger reciting Italian, and I absentmindedly praised him for his pronunciation, which was coming along nicely. Roger then spoke firmly to me in English: "Liz, could you put that newspaper down for a second? Do you have any idea what I just said?"

I looked over and noticed a very clammy boy who had a strange involuntary twitch going on his left cheek and happened to be down on one knee by my side. "No, Sweetie. Remember, I'm in charge of learning French, and you're in charge of the Italian." He began his speech again. Italian is a beautiful, musical, poetic language, but it is Greek to me. At one point I made out the phrase "Sposami, Elisabetta," and I noted the nervous tic and kneeling position, and then out came the little blue box from somewhere in his swim trunks, and things began to dawn on me . . . all my sick brain could think of was my greasy hair, bad breath, and the dirty sweats I was wearing, and there was this silent scream going in my head: *"Stop! This is not how I pictured it!"*

He opened the box, and there was this beautiful marquis-cut diamond, framed by two pear-shaped sapphires, and he looked like such a nervous wreck, so unlike himself, that I just put my arms out and hugged him. He immediately broke free of my clutches and shouted, *"What is your answer?"*

I'm afraid my exact words were something like, "Of course, you dope!" Very romantic. And then he put the ring on my finger and jumped impulsively overboard into the icy waters of the San Francisco Bay to calm his facial twitch. My first impulse was to join him, but then I looked down at this gorgeous thing on my finger, and my hand was trembling, and I thought if this ring were to slip off my finger and into the sea, I would surely die. We had more grappa to seal the deal and rushed off to spread the news. It turned out Rog had created this beautiful ring, made from his grandmother's diamond, weeks ago, and it had been burning a hole in his pocket for a good ten days, just waiting for me to be a little nicer to him so he could make his fancy Italian speech.

Now that we were engaged, we needed to connect with a church to get our plans in gear. Roger had been raised in the Episcopal Church. His mother had signed him up to be an altar boy, which meant that, as the tallest boy, he had the honor of carrying a large cross down the aisle, after which he would pretend to take his seat in an obscure alcove off the altar, then sneak out to the parking lot and spin wheelies in the family station wagon with abandon. The sermons used to make him squirm. He described the elderly priest with the thick measured English accent as the voice of God himself. Roger's mother had asked this utterly serious, slightly intimidating holy man if he could refer us to someone in Santa Barbara (where we wanted to be married) who would be willing to perform our ceremony. He arranged for a friend from seminary who worked in Santa Barbara to officiate and then invited us over to his home for a little session of premarital counseling. Roger was rattled, anticipating having to answer questions about how often we had been to church together (twice) and being probed for various other potentially embarrassing confessions. As we tentatively entered the grand staircase to the priest's home, we found ourselves in a room full of antique furniture, altars everywhere, and museum-quality paintings of Jesus, Mary, and various saints. The room was softly lit and inviting.

Father Wilder offered us a drink, which we gratefully accepted, and he proceeded to pour us each a very heavy-handed vodka tonic. Truth serum, we thought. I found Father Wilder very easy to talk to. He seemed genuinely interested in us, asking us casual questions about our day, what we did for fun, how we met, what we did last weekend. We told him we liked to get into Roger's ancient VW convertible on weekends, put the top down, and just do some joyriding. I think our drinks may have been refreshed, and suddenly the fifty-year age and experience differential between us vaporized, and the formal lines of his black suit with the starched white collar began to blur, and we began to discuss the meaning of life. As he reflected on his eighty-plus years on this earth, he said "There are many sacraments . . . the sacrament of Communion, the sacrament of baptism, the sacrament of marriage. They are all important, but too many people miss the sacredness of the simple things, the sacrament of the moment," he called it. He liked hearing that Roger brought me flowers for no reason . . . that we knew the value of a good walk on the beach together . . . and shared a love for great music. "It sounds like you two get it."

He gave us his blessing for a long and happy life, and we all realized we were starving, so we invited him out for dinner in Haight-Ashbury at this kitschy Caribbean restaurant we loved called Cha-Cha-Cha. We had forgotten that the colorful decor featured a wide variety of those cheesy religious paintings on velvet that you can get at the Tijuana border crossing—quite a contrast to his incredible art collection. We had a great evening together and couldn't help noticing that we drew quite a few stares, toasting each other with sangria, with this refined, elegant man in his priestly garb. It probably was one of the odder sights seen that evening in the Haight, a neighborhood that prides itself on its odd sights.

We got an early call the next morning from Roger's mother who had just spoken to Father Wilder. He had told her, "I had the most delightful evening with the children last night. They took me to dinner at a restaurant I don't think most of my parishioners would think to take me. I believe it was called the Club Cha-Cha." She was understandably horrified and needed an explanation, I'm sure imagining all of us in some strip club in the Tenderloin. Father Wilder died not long after that, but I have held on to his words and told his story so many times. What precious wisdom he imparted. And after that night, Roger was not one bit scared of him anymore.

One of the most cherished schemes Coco and I shared was the notion of connecting my spinster sister Meredith with her husband's best friend, Jim. But it seemed that every time Mere was here on a layover, Jim was on a business trip, and with all the craziness of planning a wedding and a six-week honeymoon, it was looking like it would have to wait until we returned from all that. Unfortunately, upon returning from our honeymoon, we were greeted with the news that Coco and her husband were being transferred back to New York. There was just enough time for one memorable dinner at their home in Mill Valley, and then to pack and say goodbye. I remember there was a big black dog that stalked Coco those last days of packing. She could hardly concentrate because she was so distracted by those big brown orphan puppy eyes, and she spent hours papering the town with "Found Dog" flyers.

A few days after Coco arrived in New York, she pulled over on the side of the road to check her map and was sideswiped by a U-Haul truck. We got the news that she was severely injured and in the hospital, possibly paralyzed. We knew she'd make it and that even if she was paralyzed, she would still shine. But one morning at the end of that week, she up and died, only thirty-three. My darling new husband, my sister Mere, and I all called in sick that day and just held on tight. I had never seen Roger cry like that. *AM San Francisco* was on TV for background noise, and they were doing a demonstration on how to brush your dog's teeth. They had poached a cute little pooch from the pound for this humiliating segment, and it was all too much for us to witness this in our grief, so when they announced that "Freckles needs a good home," we all looked at each other and said, "We have got to go save Freckles for Coco." And we did.

Jim organized the memorial service for Coco at a beautiful spot on Mount Tamalpais overlooking the ocean at sunset. Everyone told their favorite stories about her and tried to be brave. I couldn't do it. I kept thinking about that stray black dog that was so drawn to her in the days before she moved, and it just seemed like it instinctively knew something was up in that mysterious way that the animal kingdom possesses, and didn't want her to leave . . . just like me. But no one needed to hear that story, so I sat there silently and sullenly. Finally, her darling husband stood up. He said that he hadn't intended to make a speech, but he was so moved by all the things he heard that he wanted to say thank you. He went on to say how he and Coco used to love to come to this spot to watch the sunset—and maybe kill a bottle of champagne—and then to linger and watch for shooting stars. And it struck him that her life was just like one of those shooting stars . . . brilliant and bright and rare and over much too soon.

That did me in. Everyone seemed to rally to party and talk for hours. I lamely tried to fit in. I'd had a beer or two, and I remember introducing Jim to my sister in probably the messiest and most awkward way imaginable: "You know, Coco always wanted you two to meet." They both stared back at me, absolutely horrified. Rather than inflict myself on anyone else, I skulked off and found a quiet spot on the mountain and just wailed with God over the loss of her beautiful life for a good solid hour or so. Finally, I found my husband in the darkness and asked him to cart my exhausted self home.

We were driving down Green Street near the Russian Embassy. When you find yourself cresting one of those steep San Francisco hills, you'll notice the horizon of the sky is perfectly framed in the windshield just before you drop off. As we looked out toward the Berkeley hills, surrounded by all the lights of the city, we were stunned to see a star shooting across the sky. It was so bright it seemed more like a comet, with a real tail streaking behind it so we couldn't blink and miss it. I looked over at Rog, and he looked at me, and I said, "Did you see that?" He did. In my emotional state I would have been all too quick to insist that I was hallucinating without his back-up affirmation. It was Coco . . . and she was flying high. When I shared this story with her husband later, I could tell that there was a hint of doubt. He wrote me that he hoped I really did see what I said I did . . . that he had been hoping for some kind of a sign that she was okay. Her sisters, Tink and Martha, loved hearing the story, and they have since become two treasured friends. And another miracle came out of the ruins: Jim and my sister found a more appropriate time to flirt and were married two years later.

Go, Coco, go!

*"Perhaps they are not the stars at all, but rather openings in Heaven, where the light of our lost ones shines down to let us know they are with us."*

I don't know who the author of the above sentiment is, but a friend sent it to me in a card when my friend Mary died, and it really made me think of Coco and Mom. It's as if each time we are called to mourn, our loved ones who have passed on come back with a vengeance and join in.

I don't even have a photograph of Coco. Every time I see one, her natural radiance still haunts me. Her sister Tink showed me one photo I would love to have that says it all. It was taken at her memorial service. There was a surreal sunset, on a perfect bluff overlooking the Pacific Ocean on Mount Tamalpais. Sometimes the wind off the ocean will hush as if in reverence at the setting sun, holding its breath in solemn awe of the passing of day into night . . . as it was that day . . . just a hint of a warm breeze to carry the tributes of a hundred friends gathered to share their love and memories of her. Jim spoke first as the organizer of the gathering, and my mind leaped to the day Coco introduced us, one night after work in the bar across the street from our office . . . it was the day the stock market had its big crash, and as a bonds trader, Jim had been determined that night to drown his worldly grief in beer. He seemed so different to me now, facing real grief . . . his posture, his voice, his broken heart . . . and I loved him for that.

A picture was snapped just as he finished speaking . . . he had just turned to sit down . . . in the foreground were a hundred blue and white helium balloons that we each held, in the background a dizzying Technicolor sunset. Next to Jim was a bright white light . . . just the size of a human figure . . . a blip in photo processing? A reflection off the water? Coincidence?

Several different people from different points on the mountain had taken that same picture, and the light of Coco's presence was in each one . . . and it remains with all of us so blessed to have known her. God speaks so surely and truly to my heart in such mysterious moments. The first time I lost someone I loved, I tried vainly to lean on God to get through it but was so overwhelmed by the weight of grief, I mentally disconnected from God for a season. People counseled that it would all get better with time, and now I find Coco bringing me back home to God where I least expected it . . . it reminds me of that "Footprints in the Sand" poem: *"It was then that I carried you."*

It seems like such a cliché to shake one's fist at heaven in the throes of grief and demand a sign that your loved one is okay, but I am so grateful for that poetic affirmation from God that Coco is indeed alive and well and at peace and at play in the heavens. I so clearly remember how months of angst after Mom died was met with stubborn silence. And then a few months after Roger and I were married, we went to stay at my godmother's house in Fresno when we went down there to attend John Wood and Karen Krebs's wedding. She told me that she couldn't sleep at all the night she learned Mom had died, so she got up and went into her daughter's old room. Her daughter had been away at college for years, but she had never gotten around to disconnecting the telephone in that room, especially since somehow my mom had gotten that number written down in her phone book and it had become kind of her hotline. My godmother told me that phone never rang anymore, unless it was my mother. As she cried and grieved the shocking news that Mom was gone that first night, she was thinking over and over in her mind, "I've just got to know that you're all right." And then she told me that the phone did this strange, unearthly, soft purring kind of ring, just twice . . . and it both took her breath away and calmed her down so she could get some sleep. She said she hadn't told me sooner because she didn't want to upset me. I would have felt so cheated if she hadn't.

---

Back now to our story of the young lovers who were new dog owners needing to move to a place with a yard . . . no easy task in San Francisco. One Sunday afternoon we just dared ourselves to check out the cheapest open houses advertised in Marin County. The first house we saw was on a very noisy, busy corner and actually a little more than we thought we could afford. The second house was $20,000 cheaper, and we thought we should just go there for a laugh. It was an adorable fixer-upper, less than a thousand square feet. Originally built as a vacation cottage, it had a wraparound deck, nestled in huge trees, and the only thing that could be remotely considered a bedroom was this long, narrow sleeping porch that felt like it belonged in a tree house. The bathroom had a gigantic claw-foot tub just perfect for two long, lanky geeks. Eureka!

We didn't care that Roger couldn't even stand up straight anywhere in the entire downstairs and that there didn't appear to be any closets. We quickly figured that with 20 percent down plus the tax deductions, our monthly mortgage payments would be less than our rent in the city. My amazing dad volunteered to help us with the down payment since we had just spent all our money on our honeymoon. Dad had been keeping his cash in conservative CDs, and we were able to pay him a much better interest rate than he was getting there, and everybody was happy. The house was so tiny, we figured we would stay there a couple of years at the most and build up equity to buy a real house. It was there that we discovered the joys of being young and poor and in love. We lived so lean that we often wondered if we were going to be able to pay our bills. Our entertainment on the weekends would consist of a cheap six-pack of beer and a crowbar and a sledgehammer or a paintbrush. I remember having a couple of beers one Friday night, and it seemed like a great idea to demolish the false ceiling in our kitchen, and we uncovered this great original beadboard ceiling, and then fell giggling into that bathtub together exhausted and elated. In our little love shack, we ended up conceiving both babies and lived there happily for five years.

When I first suspected I was pregnant, times were especially lean—I hadn't had a commission check in months, and I was more than a little hesitant to break the news to my husband. I used to wake up in a recurring nightmarish cold sweat and think, *"Oh my gosh, I'm pregnant!"* and then I'd roll over and see my husband sleeping there and think, "It's okay. I'm married."

I got a call one day around that time from Coco's husband telling me that he was moving back to San Francisco, and he wanted me to find him a condo. The poor guy got more than he bargained for; we spent hours together looking at property and reminiscing and sobbing a lot about Coco. And then, a couple of months before I was due to deliver our baby, he revised his request and told me he thought he was going to need a house instead, because his new girlfriend was also pregnant, and they were going to get married and come out to San Francisco together. As if offering a cold compress to a shock victim, he said, "Once you've been happily married, it's almost impossible to go back to being single." He chose to move on and love again as a tribute to the beautiful love story he had shared with Coco. They made an offer on a rambling Edwardian home the day I had the baby, providing me with a generous commission to buffer my maternity leave, and went on to have four children together in that house.

# Falling in Love . . . All by Myself

A serious miracle would have been needed for either one of the spinster Koenig sisters to fall in love, and that is just what God had in mind when he moved Roger W. Krakow Jr. into the available studio apartment downstairs. We literally had to trip over him whenever we came or went anywhere, so our friendship evolved naturally. He was just a great guy . . . funny and easygoing and cute and really tall. I wish I could say it was love at first sight, but in fact, in my own shallow way, I actually tried to set him up with my good friend Carey, who is six feet tall, knowing that as tall people they would have so much in common. They could commiserate on all those "How's the weather up there?" jokes! I had been dating a friend of Carey's from high school for a record six months or so. He was a sweet guy, very kind, but I kind of had a vague feeling I was a bit too much for him sometimes. In fact, when I suggested we take a short break to see if we missed each other, I swear I heard an audible sigh of relief, and he never called me again. Anyway, I introduced Carey and Roger at a party at our apartment, they chatted for five or ten minutes, and then Carey marched straight over to me and said, "What are you doing? He is so perfect for *you*!"

It was as if a ton of bricks had fallen from heaven and clocked me over the head, and I suddenly got it. I could see my destiny. I think I fell in love that very night. Hard. All by myself. Carey, by the way, met and married a guy a full head shorter not long after that. Go figure.

The bloom of newfound love helped me become uncharacteristically bold. I ordered up six tickets for the Berkeley Shakespeare Festival's production of *A Midsummer Night's Dream* for our casual first outing with four other friends. I was absolutely swept away by the story of other like-minded fools for love and afterward steered our little party over to Berkeley's Rose Garden to howl at the moon and drink a bottle of port. It was a perfect evening. Sure, there was that awkward moment when we approached the front door to our mutual apartments . . . long pause . . . Roger claims to this day that he had no idea we were on a date. He idiotically thought we were six friends going to see a play. How *dense* can a person be? He finally invited me in and said, "See all this, Liz?" What I saw was a small studio complete with queen-sized bed topped with red flannel down comforter, a piano beside the bed, a large desk with a computer in the kitchen, one of those shiny burlwood bachelor-chic coffee tables topped with a stereo, and a fireplace beneath a large antique elk head with antlers covered in twinkly lights. "This is a shrine to my independence!" He went on to tell me that he had been living with a woman for the past three years, and it hadn't worked out. This new bachelor pad was the ultimate sanctuary for him.

"I like your elk head," I said. "You know, my initials are E-L-K." Go, gal, go! Mark your territory! He then totally charmed me by opening the stack of mail piled high on his piano. From this I could see that he gave to the Sierra Club, Green Peace, KQED, Amnesty International, Habitat for Humanity, UNICEF, and the Special Olympics. How cute is that? Today he claims he was trying to bore me enough so I would go home so he could get some sleep in his little shrine to his independence. All I could think of was that Donnie Hathaway was singing "Misty" there on the stereo, and when the heck was he going to ask me to dance or maybe give me a little kiss? At some point I recall I just glommed on to him, and we had a quick dance, and I went home . . . confused and alone as usual. In the weeks to come, I burned up the pages of my journal with all the fury and drama of unrequited true love. I pursued my passion with a vengeance that today would probably be called stalking. Here is a journal entry fresh from that tortured era:

> I have just fallen in love! Utterly and profoundly in love! And once again the guy has no clue. But this feeling right now is enough . . . it's like being struck by lightning . . . it's a magical, mysterious current of energy that sort of originates at the sun and then bounces off the moon and can actually pierce the cold loneliness in that dungeon where you've kept your heart all those years . . . and you're standing there naked and trembling in the darkness but not the least bit cold or scared or embarrassed even because there are a zillion new stars in the sky that you've never even noticed before and they're swirling around your head and lighting your way at the same time . . . and so you sing a psalm of praise to God as Cupid and marvel that he didn't forget after all to create that one quirky person with whom you could forge magic . . . that you could love in your own pathetic way . . . even if he still thinks you're just one heck of a friendly neighbor and that's all thankyouverymuch.

Good grief.

My spinster sister had recently taken on a job as a flight attendant so that she could travel the world for free, unfortunately based out of Detroit, so I took in my precious former Berkeley roommate Anne Murphy on a permanent basis. My sister promised to jet in from Motown at every available opportunity. Anne was a law student at Hastings Law School, which was very demanding, and I had a lot of time on my hands. Danger. I found myself doing a lot of laundry and being especially conscientious about taking out the trash, both of which caused me to traipse past Roger's doorway and hopefully catch a glimpse of my one true love. I was not above standing on the sidewalk below his window spying and humming the tune "Knowing I'm on the Street Where You Live" to myself. Tuesday night was poker night at his shrine to his independence. There were always five or six guys, all single, drinking beer, smoking cigars, and having a big old noisy time. I found that endearing, because I, too, was always in my element with a gang of my best girlfriends gathered around me.

It made me feel like we were kindred spirits—perhaps just late bloomers in the love department. One Tuesday night the door was standing open, so I could say hi, and he invited Anne and me to come over for a fish fry on Friday night. I could hardly contain my glee.

That night I had a dream about my mom for the first time in ages. She and Woody Allen were conspiring to plan my wedding. Woody was like Franck, Martin Short's wedding planner in *Father of the Bride*, and he was hired chiefly to make sure my wedding would be classified a comedy. My sister dreams about our mother often—funny, ordinary anecdotes where they just sort of touch base with each other in the middle of the night. I'd been so jealous that I seemed to be unable to enjoy such reunions. But that night my mind suddenly felt free to dream again. Something about finally meeting a man I could imagine sharing my wildest dreams with and already the "m-word" is seeping into my subconscious . . . I could see Roger making my mom laugh the way Woody Allen movies make all of us laugh (this was before he personally became so unfunny). I suppose I should say all that in the past tense, but her spirit continues to play little tricks on me to remind me she is still very much a part of the present. Just that morning I found one of her silver seashell earrings taped to the bathroom door at work. It wasn't even sterling silver—neither one of us could ever hold on to material possessions of any value (and therefore never wanted much to do with them)—but the sentimental fact of losing even a token part of her had gotten me down. They were clip-ons, and I had lost one or the other of them many times before. This time, I'd been sure the earring was gone, but it appeared again, as mysteriously as she had disappeared all those years ago.

I'll never forget that phone call, from fifteen hundred miles away from home . . . my father's sad, quivering voice asking me if I was alone . . . I was, of course. Mom had died instantly of a heart attack—with her boots on, helping my brother, her last born, move into his college dorm. She had launched us all and moved on to bigger and better things.

Her funeral was the most surreal day. The first impulse had been to scatter her ashes at sea because she was truly a mermaid at heart. I liked to refer to her as the Mer-Mom . . . she was always at her happiest with dogs and babies on the beach, "with a bit of a cold wind always at her back," as one of her best friends once said. She loved that comment, and I love to think of her that way. One of her favorite books was Anne Morrow Lindbergh's *A Gift from the Sea*:

*The sea does not reward those who are too anxious, too greedy or too impatient.*
*To dig for treasures shows not only impatience and greed, but lack of faith.*
*Patience, patience, patience. Patience and faith. That's what the sea teaches.*
*One should lie open and choiceless as a beach—waiting for a gift from the sea.**

But on second thought, we weren't ready or willing to let her just vaporize. We wanted that physical, grassy spot with a vase for daisies and something sentimental etched beneath her name. When we were kids, she used to drag us through ancient cemeteries on family vacations, charmed by the poetry and artistry and history behind each headstone. On hers we wrote, "Love like a warm sea breeze, filling our sails and opening our horizons to all that is beautiful." A little sappy but straight from the heart. She probably would think it too heavy an epitaph, but then she never did give herself much credit or take herself too seriously. I can still see the Mer-Mom tearing across the Victoria overpass, which runs along the cemetery—Mer-dog in the copilot seat of the blue VW van, three (!) bored teenagers in the back—and she was feeling frisky: "When I die, I want to be buried right down there so you kids can drive by and honk and toss your beer cans at me!"

Memories like that amused us as we lingered on that spot after her funeral, trying hard not to wallow in our sadness. A beat-up car with three boys about our ages rolled up with a Frisbee, a dog, and a twelve-pack of Coors. We started talking to them after a while, and it turned out that they had just buried their father that morning. After moping around, they asked themselves what their dad would want them to do, and they got creative. We shared our beer can story and found many other things in common: Each parent had died on the same day, suddenly, of a heart attack . . . both out of town in Santa Barbara.

---

* Anne Morrow Lindbergh, *Gift From The Sea*, New York: Pantheon Books, 1955, p. 11.

The more we talked, the more we noticed similarities in values, spirit, and joie de vivre in the ways we were all raised—and in the way we were trying to cope with loss. I know it sounds strange, but it was just the kind of coincidence (definition: God performing miracles anonymously) that brings comfort. We were survivors, but we were not alone . . . and we felt peace knowing that their dad and our mom were up there having a good laugh and maybe a beer together. We left a thoughtful arrangement of beer cans when we finally left that night.

But I digress. All that goes a long way to describe the needy, love-starved atmosphere poor Roger stumbled into unwittingly when he moved into his shrine to his independence, just next door and downstairs from the spinster sisters and Anne Murphy. When you lose one of the people you love most in the world, there is just this gigantic void left behind. But it also left me with a kind of crazed urgency about living, knowing that I was exactly half the age my mom was when she died, and since she had already gotten married and pregnant by my age, I had better figure things out and quick since my life was suddenly probably half over before it even started if you do the math!

I truly believe that death can be very life affirming. It is tempting to feel like a giant chunk of you has died, too, because it is just so physically painful, even potentially contagious. I would wake up each morning pinching myself, incredulous to discover that I was, in fact, alive. Being alive is an awesome thing. I don't think I had ever really noticed before. Every ending is also a beginning, an awakening. I had this whole new vision of what was left of my life and what it could be. I wanted it so bad I could taste it, and God help that dense neighbor of mine who might foil my evil plans. *Hahahahahha*!

Back to that Friday-night fish fry . . . Roger had been up in Idaho shooting a video documentary on a salmon-trout farm, and had returned with four gigantic, beautiful fish. Right out of the gates, the intimate dinner party I had romantically envisioned turned out to be a scene of about twenty people in his cozy little studio/independence shrine. A tall, thin brunette babe seemed to be lurking a little too closely to my true love. (I later learned that they had gone to a Bruce Springsteen concert together the week before.)

Further complicating my plan for the evening, a nice guy at the party began making the moves on *me*! Could it be that no one else in the room could see what my friend Carey had so clearly seen that fateful night: that Roger was perfect for *me and only me*? Apparently, the tall, thin brunette was perceptive enough to feel the poison darts that shot out from my eyes whenever she got too close to Roger, and to her credit, she left the party early.

My new roommate, Anne Murphy, was easily the most brilliant, soulful, wonderfully original woman I have ever known, and I felt so lucky to get to live with her. We could get completely lost in endless conversations about the meaning of life, politics, sex, religion . . . all the taboos. Conversations like those are what I most miss now in my harried suburban life of duty and so much minutiae. In college we were famous for our road trips to football games, volleyball tournaments, any excuse not to study. She was so brilliant she could just show up for the finals and get A's. She graduated a full semester early. We should have died a thousand deaths together—actually, we were fond of mocking death. She had this awful trench coat we called the death-coat that she would wear over her gray death-sweats whenever we would duck out for a nightcap at the nearby Darling Durant Hotel bar in Berkeley. Anne always insisted on buying a round with the emergency credit card her dad had given her, since neither of us ever had any actual money. She also liked to wear these really heavy black clogs, which truly were death-clogs, because every single time she hopped into them, she was guaranteed to fall off them.

I remember one road trip in her hatchback VW death-car (aptly named for the way it piped exhaust fumes into the car for all of us to breathe), heading south to the UCLA football game. There were five of us crammed into it for a six-hour ride. We were about halfway there in a desolate area of Central California that has been known ever since as the Death-Triangle, just south of King City and north of Paso Robles. We were all a little woozy from the death-car fumes, and I swear I looked down and saw the death-clogs on the floor of the car with this scary visible steam emanating from them . . . perhaps reacting to the carbon monoxide that was being piped in. In a knee-jerk reaction that I pretended to regret, I reached down and threw them out the window, somewhere near San Ardo, risking the wrath of Murph. She forgave me because I think she truly feared them herself.

Since then, however, there has been a remarkable rash of car-related calamities in the Death-Triangle, and I can only blame the death-clogs that still roam there. When my parents came up for my college graduation, they drove their VW van up and tragically blew the engine there in the Triangle near Los Banos (Spanish for "the toilets") on their return trip. It took weeks to get parts shipped in, and the van never quite hummed the same again. Clunkity-clop. Clunkity-clop.

A few months later, I was traveling alone from Monterey to Ventura for the wedding of my oldest friend, Joani, and I cracked the block on my Toyota near San Ardo, which is so *nowhere* that it is in fact the heart of the Triangle, where the only gas station is always closed, and the pay phone vandalized. I spent the better part of the day on the side of the road waiting for a policeman or anyone to stop and help me, and I vividly felt the relentless specter of the death-clogs stalking me and clearly preventing any do-gooder from stopping to help. Clunkity-clop. Clunkity-clop. I swear I was in the twilight zone that day. After a good four hours of absolute desperation without seeing even one policeman go by—remember the days before cell phones?—I was able to safely hitchhike south, just before dark, with a man who was so unbelievably kind, so not an axe murderer, to the nearest motel, the Cinderella Motel, a memorable little sanctuary about a half hour away in Paso Robles. Mom drove up and bailed me out the next morning, hauling me to the wedding just in time, and I was car-less for weeks. Later that year Anne's own death-car coughed, sputtered, and spontaneously combusted on the side of the road, perilously near the Triangle. Coincidence? I think not. Beware the death-clogs of the apocalypse. Clunkity-clop.

One afternoon during our last quarter together before Anne graduated from Cal, I came home from class to change clothes into something darling before my Berkeley Chorus practice, as was my habit since I'd developed a fierce crush on its dreamy Italian conductor. I found Anne and her roommate,

Deb, moping on the bed with an open bottle of Jack Daniel's. Deb's heart had been broken by this dude that she'd been certain she'd been waiting for all her life, and so we shared a couple of shots for tea and sympathy. Suddenly, I looked at my watch and realized I had to run—no time to change out of my sweats—or I would miss choir practice, which I could not imagine doing since it had totally fueled my rich fantasy life in the boy-deprived doldrums of that senior year. Who needed boys anyway? This was a real man. And I was one of a hundred anonymous altos and sopranos singing adoringly to him every Tuesday and Thursday afternoon. Well, not exactly anonymous. I'm afraid I had distinguished myself in my own special way.

I knew that with Anne graduating early, I would need to find an alternative creative outlet to survive my senior year. Ever since my successful (!) run with the Melekalikimaka Good-Time Band, I had missed having music in my life, and my friend Melissa had dared me to check out the UC Berkeley Chorus auditions on a lark. I popped my head into the classroom and found a dashing young conductor sitting at the piano, just wrapping up auditions. He invited me to audition, and I said I hadn't anything prepared and tried to leave.

"Oh, you must know something. How about something patriotic?" His seductive Italian accent sucked me in against my better judgment.

"Sure! How about 'America the Beautiful'? 'The Star-Spangled Banner'?" I suggested.

What went down from there was a bit of a blur . . . I know I was loud, flat, and very enthusiastic. My late-adolescent hormones were kind of surging just being alone in a room with this dreamboat of a man, and it was all just enough to swirl my brain into producing the strangest combination of lyrics imaginable. I vaguely recall that I sort of hybridized the two songs into something I'll call "America the Ugly Meets the Star-Mangled Banner." The lovely professor struggled to suppress his amusement.

"Do you read music?" he asked politely.

"I took piano lessons for a few years," I replied lamely.

"Come here; let's see how you do."

I stood behind him trying to read the music to this "Virga Jesse floruit" Latin ditty and just bombed. Sometimes I amaze even myself how little common sense I possess. What on earth in me thought I could bluff my way through this audition in front of this highly accomplished music scholar, I will never know.

"Can you make an additional sectional class on Wednesday afternoons?" he asked.

"Sure," I said.

"We'll try to put some notes in you then."

I slid gratefully out of the room, full of the strangest combination of giddy elation and abject mortification. Those choral practices were a highlight for me each week, but I honestly could never again quite meet his eyes. I felt so totally transparent and idiotic around him. If he so much as said hello to me, I would go into a full-body blush and my tongue would get thick, and I could never be sure what inane thing might fly out of my mouth. But on that one fateful day that bottle of Jack Daniel's had relaxed my tongue, and I ran out of the house like a madwoman to be on time for chorus. For some reason, I must have had enough to drink that I was unable to tell time properly, and I arrived ten minutes early instead of late. Drat . . . I really could have used that time to change out of my sweats after all! The auditorium was empty. I decided to hike up into the dark far rear rows to hide out with my liquored-up breath, messy hair stuffed into a baseball cap, and oversized sweatpants. Out of nowhere, the beautiful maestro seemed to just materialize and made a beeline right toward me, just as I was feeling so sure I was invisible.

"Have you been playing tennis?" he inquired.

"Yes! Tennis!" I enthused.

"Are you any good?" he asked.

"I used to compete in high school," I said, careful not to slur my words.

"We should play sometime . . . how about Friday?" he asked.

Just like that. I walked on air that week. When we finally played tennis, I was weirdly competitive with him. It was as if tennis was my only hope of leveling the vast differential in the life-experience playing field between us. I'd studied his every move all year long and had placed him on such a pedestal. He was so creative and brilliant and accomplished and worldly. We played three all-out sets (and he won all three), and then I had to quit, due to a massive exploded blister on my hand. I was glad for it, as it provided me a face-saving excuse for not giving him a better game, and when I showed him the festering sore, he took my hand and gave it a tender kiss and said, "Why didn't you say to quit sooner?" And then he offered to buy me a beer. And we began a flirtation that went way beyond my wildest daydreams, yet at the same time, was remarkably chaste when you consider all that Italian blood rushing through his veins, and, oh I forgot to mention, it turned out he was married.

But I think this quasi-romantic interlude with someone I so revered helped me begin to see myself as a functioning human being beyond the safe confines of college life. In June he offered all graduating seniors positions in the San Francisco Opera Chorus for the summer, which was totally surreal. I remember the performances involved a cast of thousands for *Aida* and *Die Meistersinger von Nürnberg*, the latter being a five-hour epic, with me in the crowd scenes wearing a large orange wool dress that seemed to weigh more than I did, festooned with a hat that could only be described as an upside-down bucket with streamers flowing from it. On the night of one performance—I remember it was my twenty-second birthday—the maestro had offered to leave tickets for my parents, who understandably had to see me, of the flat/tone-deaf Koenigs, performing in the SF Opera Chorus, to believe it. He called me up to his office just before going on stage and gave me a beautiful book of W. H. Auden's poetry to wish me a happy birthday, with the note: "Read the 'New Year's Letter.'" And then he kissed me full on the lips and sent me on stage, where I was supposed to be able to remember how to sing in German for five hours after all that.

After a few hours of the performing ordeal, the gal next to me in the crowd scene promptly fainted under the strain of that hot summer night, which was such a rip-off since that was exactly what I had been thinking of doing, as I stood there singing, emoting grandly and sweating buckets in my bucket hat, which was now resting on the bridge of my nose. I could distinctly hear my mother's voice carrying across the packed house, just howling with gut-wrenching laughter in all the wrong places. She didn't speak German, and I had clearly neglected to tell her it was *not* a comedy.

Anne went back to Washington, DC, to work in politics after graduation, and I went into fundraising for nonprofits, ending up in Boulder, Colorado, where I had banished my potentially home-wrecking self to a life of service and penance. We reconnected again when her dear father became terminally ill with cancer, and she came home again. I remember he died on Valentine's Day, and I was home at my parents' for a visit. Anne had taken a break from her intense bedside vigil the day before and come up to my parents' house to sit on the patio and have a beer, which had always been good medicine for us up until then. I remember feeling like I didn't know what to say to her—it was all such a dreaded nightmare—and thinking all I was good for was to try to lighten things up a bit. I remember really noticing my mom relate to her that day. She was very insightful and brave, and I wondered how she knew what to do with this situation, since it seemed to me she had never lost anyone close to her before. She was beautiful and wise and a marvel, and I was proud of her. Six months later she was also dead, so Anne and I got to be death-friends too.

Anne had always wanted to be a lawyer like her dad, and I had always cherished the lofty ambition of living in San Francisco. When she first started Hastings Law School in San Francisco, a year or so after my sister and I found our apartment, she could only afford a dreary basement apartment with three other starving students. Her room was actually more like a hallway for the other roommates to walk through. I went over one day and made her some curtains for a little privacy, but I could hardly stand to see her live like that. She was so into studying she seemed to be unaware that there was never any food or (God forbid) beer in the fridge. I took it upon myself to launch a "Save Murph-the-Serf" fundraising campaign. I mailed a letter out to everyone I could think of, with a little coupon at the bottom that you could clip off and send back, checking off the appropriate box:

I would like to donate the equivalent of a 6-pack of Coors ___$2.99.
I would like to donate the equivalent of a 6-pack of Guinness ___$5.99.
I would like to donate a suitcase of Wiedemann's ___$1.88.

Imagine her delight when the checks began rolling in! (She wanted to kill me.)

A year later when she was able to move into my posh yet affordable digs with a sideways view out to the Golden Gate Bridge, I was able to spoil her with a constant supply of cheap gallon jugs of wine. Today she is a shameless wine snob, and I never tire of bringing these stories up whenever I am allowed to meet her fancy new friends.

I had a great job then that paid dirt, but I didn't care. I handled the publicity for a supper club atop Nob Hill. I got to ride around in limousines with extraordinary talents like James Brown, Gregory Hines, B. B. King, and Ella Fitzgerald, escorting them to radio and TV interviews. I remember spending an amazing afternoon connecting with Gregory Hines, who was newly married and really into talking about love and romance, and then he asked me to tell him all about my old man, so I rhapsodized on and on about Roger, carefully omitting the fact that our love affair was still taking place pretty much completely all in my mind. He was such a lovely multitalented man, and I still can't quite believe that cancer could have caught up with him so young. My favorite story from this era was the incredible day I got to spend with B. B. King. We had hours together, heading over to the old KJAZ radio station in Oakland and then back again in the back seat of a limousine. I was hanging on his every word by the end of the day; he was just so wonderful to be with. As we were saying goodbye, he said to me, "You know, Liz, if I were a younger, better-looking man, I'd try to marry you." I told him he was the sweetest man I'd ever met and the first to even joke about the m-word with me. Did my battered ego a world of good.

If it were possible to find anyone more clueless about love than my spinster sister or me, even Murph would have to admit it was she. She appointed herself my love broker and took it upon herself to make sure Roger came to see that I was indeed his destiny. After that strategic first fish fry, we invited Roger to come by the next night for pasta and to watch *Annie Hall* on TV. The movie was half over when he finally stopped by. We had almost given up on him and had dipped into the cheap wine to attempt to anesthetize our romantically pulverized hearts, when my one true love finally arrived at our apartment. There was nothing left of the bottle to offer him, so we had to open up this really nice bottle of port that we had been saving for a special occasion. I'm sure by now you are thinking that we were hopeless raging alcoholics. It's just that we were both such high-strung control freaks that I firmly believe that without dabbling in the sauce as we did, there would have been no possible way to get around the elaborate security/sabotage systems we had unknowingly erected around our hearts. That bottle of port was pure romance . . . to this day the mere mention of the word *port* can put me in the mood for love.

Anne and I were supposed to leave the next afternoon for a camping trip to Yosemite, where we planned to meet up with all the members of her gigantic, wonderful Irish-Catholic family, and she boldly invited Rog to join us. Under the influence of port, it seemed like a great idea. She then announced with an elaborate flourish that she was leaving the two of us alone. Every five minutes or so she would pop her head out of her bedroom door and announce that she was still leaving us alone. I recall brazenly asking Rog if he would like a back rub, and at that point I think it may have dawned on him at last that I wanted to be more than his friendly neighbor.

I don't think it would be exaggerating to say that it was one of the all-time great high school make-out sessions of all time. I don't mean to diminish the erupting passions by calling it "high school." For me there is nothing quite as euphoric as the feeling of that first passionate kiss. There is such intensity in the eye contact, and such cheap thrills in feeling the muscles in a guy's arms up close for the first time, the feel of his skin, the softness of the lips, the smell of his hair, and the forbidden thought that your parents could walk in on you at any moment. In our case, of course, there was Anne rooting for us just on the other side of that door to heighten the spectacle. But just the almost unbearable sweetness of feeling those things for the first time, flooding my body, mind, and soul was so amazing. I fear our culture's obsession with sex is in danger of completely bypassing the gorgeous sacrament of making out on the sofa. And there is something so incredibly sexy in the dance, the yearning, and the anticipation, the longing. We fogged up the windows until 3:00 or so in the morning, and then knowing we both had to work the next day before heading out to Yosemite, Rog dutifully went downstairs. He later told me he stood outside my door for a good ten minutes or so, daring himself to kick in the door and ravish me. I told him he was a baby for not doing just that.

Finally . . . after all the clever traps I'd laid for him, he was under my spell. I just couldn't believe it. We all made it to Yosemite the next day, and we camped near Lake Tuolumne. That night we found ourselves sharing a large family-sized tent with Anne and her two brothers: Jim, age twelve, and Rex, age fourteen. Every time we dared to sneak even the teensiest kiss, we would be mocked with "Oh gross! Cut that out!" But that weekend, for me, he already felt like family. It was a sweet affirmation that my instincts were right on about Roger . . . I could just throw him into a carnival atmosphere full of total strangers and watch the grace of his personality carry the day.

Poor Roger . . . most of what I knew about sex I learned from another neighbor, Mike Hawthorne, who lived down the street from us at the beach where we grew up. His sister was one of my best friends. She was a year older than me, and Mike was a year younger, but he spoke to me one day in the sand dunes with such authority I am confident that it laid the foundation for my complete ineptness in matters of the heart. I couldn't have been more than seven or eight years old when he told me that the man takes the woman into a dark place and puts his you-know-what in her you-know-where, and that's where babies come from. He also went on to tell me that scientists had created a bomb that could blow up the entire world, which I was able to confirm was true, so I could deduce that the other thing was probably true, and I honestly don't think I had a good night's sleep for the rest of my childhood. That messy tangle of sex and nuclear annihilation intertwined, bouncing around relentlessly in my childhood brain, made me into the basket case I am today for sure.

We all know it is common for children to fear alligators under their bed and monsters in their closets, but I just lay awake all night, every night, imagining that bomb landing right there by my bed in Ventura. And my parents were so busy with a baby and a three-year-old (and I didn't even want to imagine how they got here!) that they had precious little patience for my nighttime traumas. I was five years old when my brother arrived on the scene, and I remember acting so grown up and insisted on being treated like someone so old and responsible. He was almost like my baby. And somehow, I managed to keep up the charade that I was in fact a grown-up who didn't need anyone's help, probably until the day my mom died, and the jig was up.

My freshman year in college, I roomed with the dearest gal, Kathy, whose closest sister had been killed in one of those heinous teenage-driving accidents. She once told me I reminded her of her sister, and we bonded for life. We were both so naive that we elected to live on the only all-girl floor in our dorm, known as "the Convent," which was I think meant to be a joke, but since we both shared a love of the movie *The Sound of Music* and had no idea about the direction of our future careers, Fräulein Maria wasn't such a bad role model.

We used to read *Cosmopolitan* magazine to see what we could glean about sex. The year was 1978, and I am sure you can fact-check my story if you think I am making this up. We were reading this very scientific article on the male reproductive organ. The penis . . . there, I said it. The article said, "The average penis is 4¾" in tumescent diameter." We studiously looked up the word *tumescent* in the dictionary: "adjective: swollen or excited." We got out our protractor and drew the darn thing to scale. It was the size of a gigantic peanut butter jar, and to think that having sex would be like birthing babies every time and so clearly not worth it! It was absolutely shocking and were we ever glad that we did choose to live on the convent floor, where it was safe! Two months later we were still bravely reading *Cosmo* and were delighted to find an alert reader calling their attention to a very critical factual error. They had intended to write "tumescent circumference." But for us, the damage had been done.

As I look back, I can admit to an exhausting pattern of being attracted to emotionally unavailable men, and Roger was no exception there for a while.

That thrilling flirtation my senior year of college with the married maestro had left me with a powerful yen for someone older and wiser to take me on as a project and usher me into the mysterious world of adultness.

I had tried to throw myself into my meaningful work doing fundraising for nonprofits in Colorado right after I graduated, but it was so desperately lonely. It was a college town, and everyone that I worked with was middle aged and married, and I was lost somewhere in between for many long months. To be honest, I had to admit that I was still kind of carrying the torch for that boy who gave me those first passionate kisses back in high school. He had gone off and gotten married when he was about twenty and was divorced a year later, and I naively figured it had to be a sign that our time had finally come. We had faded in and out of each other's lives for years, always with a kind of surreal physical attraction, accompanied by a familiar regressive adolescent social awkwardness. I had just adored him since I was fifteen. We spoke the same language on paper, but when we were actually together, we couldn't communicate to save our lives . . . almost as if it stirred up those crazy-making adolescent hormones again. He once wrote me:

> Remember: we live in deeds, not in years,
> In thoughts, not in breaths,
> In feelings, not in figures on a dial.
> We should count time by heart throbs.

I still love that. When he was in business school, we would write each other wild letters and poems, and I kept a lot of them for their therapeutic value. I used to worry that his artistic side would be squashed in business school and wrote him a note: "Talk to me, my dear old friend! You have the heart and soul of a poet, and you have captured my imagination . . . we are outlaws in wingtips and practical pumps."

We both loved the Tom Robbins book *Still Life with Woodpecker*, identifying I think, with its main characters, a mad bomber and a pregnant cheerleader:

*Don't let yourself be victimized by the age you live in. It's not the times that* *will bring us down, any more than it's society. What limits people is that they don't have the fucking nerve or imagination to star in their own movie, let alone direct it. YUK.*[*]

In another letter he wrote:

> I don't want to hear about your conquests,
> Or your casual affairs.
> Each one a great story but who cares?
> I want to know about your feelings, or the ache in your heart . . .
> The thoughts that make you what you are, that set you apart.
> I come to see you often, and you know why I do.
> Because maybe you will talk about what I have felt too.
> Of things I've never told a soul because of my pride.
> And longtime fears that I keep hidden way down inside.
> And I'll know what you mean.

I remember the day he came to visit me in Boulder to go skiing . . . I was so excited that I rushed out and got a frightening new permanent in my hair that caused me to smell like rotten eggs and look exactly like Art Garfunkel's undesirable younger sister, if he had one. I honestly do not know how he coped with the toxicity . . . I personally couldn't even stand being around myself. He managed to maintain a bemused affection for me that visit as he had over the years, probably in the way Art Garfunkel would have if he'd had a socially awkward sister. Our paths would cross again and again, and we would always kiss because we were so darn good at it after all those years of practicing on and off, and for me it imprinted in my mind that this was how I'd always wanted to be kissed.

After that last brief and confusing visit when I found myself alone again in my little condo at the base of the rugged Flatiron Mountains, I wrote a lot of tortured lonely poetry inspired by yet another failed attempt at love. Here's a sample:

---

* Tom Robbins, *Still Life with Woodpecker,* Bantam Books, 1980, p. 110.

## Falling in Love . . . All by Myself

Fading in, fading out . . .
generations of affection and indifference . . .
we like magnets, attract and repel . . .
our strange, neglected embers
stubbornly linger . . .
ignited again by gusts of cold wind.
Separate wills seduced
by glittering challenges . . .
intoxicating, tangible roads
undertaken with blind bravado.
Worldly achievements prove easier . . .
but the heart is the beacon of
the road less traveled.
Tasting our dreams,
force-fed our nightmares . . .
ugly arbitrary little disasters
add layers of ice
to each heart's sequestered chamber
creating a dungeon
powerless to warm itself.
Earthbound, feet firmly on the muddied ground
as if for the first time.
I don't know how to live this way,
so I'll pack it up for a new road
this time darker, foggier . . .
not even a road, but a trench . . .
the front lines in a private cold war . . .
but you will always be in my duffel bag, Comrade.
The sky may be falling,
Chicken Little is chicken,
and Red Riding Hood needs to visit grandma . . .
remembering there is a somewhere over the rainbow

and a little engine that could.
Such are the fanciful memories
of an inordinately long childhood
that appears to have abruptly ended . . .
the fairy tale exposed . . . a fraud.

The poor, poor guy. I wrote that and mailed it off to clarify how I felt after his visit. I believe I also sent along the lyrics to that Art Garfunkel song "All I Know": "I bruise you; you bruise me . . . we both bruise too easily . . . too easily to let it show. I love you and that's all I know" . . . as if it might somehow help explain away my bizarre smelly new hairdo and my subsequent erratic behavior. That last intimate gesture may have had something to do with inspiring him to relocate himself on over to the far side of the continent, where he successfully married a truly wonderful, stable woman the following year.

A few weeks later at my first big campaign kickoff meeting there in Colorado Springs, I couldn't have been more surprised when I found myself at a big round table of forty or so middle-aged volunteers and one incredibly gorgeous hunk of the male kind. I couldn't help sneaking looks at him throughout the tedious meeting, and when he approached me and introduced himself at a break, I had a gnawing suspicion that something good might finally be happening in my life . . . or perhaps someone who seemed a lot like me. He was charming—a lobbyist for the ski industry—and he was witty, intelligent, successful, confident, worldly, generous, refined, enlightened, and very smooth . . . I could read all of this in just a few moments of looking into his penetrating blue eyes. I was guessing he was maybe twenty years older than I, which was confirmed as we chatted and got on to a tangent about him hassling with his seventeen-year-old daughter over wanting to stay up all night for the prom, and what did I think. Remembering my own prom just a few years earlier, all I could recall was that I couldn't wait to get home in my own bed that night . . . which wasn't much help. On the plus side, at least it turned out he was actually divorced.

He invited me for a drink after the meeting that night. He was staying at this grand old hotel in Colorado Springs that night because we had a series of meetings the next day. I of course was driving home two hours that night to save money like a dweeb. But we had a drink and a dance before I left, and it was all unbelievably, perfectly romantic. He went on to court me like I had never experienced before, writing me tender postcards as he traveled, and then we would meet in Denver for romantic dinners. He was very sweet and protective of me and never pushed, and I began to fear that I was under a kind of spell that was really too good to be true.

Then one night we were invited to dinner at the home of some good friends of his who lived outside of Evergreen. I sat in his kitchen, fascinated by the way he made margaritas for our road trip. He'd take an ice cube in his hand, rap it briskly with a spoon, toss the chunks into a jar full of lime juice and tequila and triple sec, and then shake it all up. I'd never seen it done like that. It turned out to be a pleasant enough evening, and I enjoyed his friends, even though when he excused himself to go to the bathroom, they felt compelled to say to me, "Do you have any idea *who* he is? Only one of the most eligible bachelors in Colorado, according to *Denver* magazine." And they proceeded to highlight his many-splendored accomplishments. Clearly the fluke of him being even remotely attracted to someone who looked like Art Garfunkel's loser twin sister (if he'd had one) did not compute for them. That night when we got back to his place, he calmly, dispassionately told me he didn't think he loved me anymore—that he had connected with an old girlfriend on his last trip. I sat there for a minute in stunned silence, just totally preoccupied with this vivid image in my head of him robotically making those margaritas earlier . . . and I felt cold and sour just like that margarita, as if he'd just rapped me over the head with his silver spoon, dead center, and tossed the perfectly broken pieces into an icy jar and screwed the lid on tight, shaking it all up real good. The pieces were all still in there, just hideously rearranged . . . and once again I felt the trapdoor of the dungeon where I kept my heart slam resolutely shut, the perennial ice in the chambers another layer thicker.

I confided the whole sordid tale to my mother, who wrote me a beautiful letter of encouragement, telling me not to worry, that I was just a late bloomer in the love department and that this man simply was not worthy of my affection. Aww, thanks, Mom!

Not long after that, the phone rang, and I heard this very sexy, deep voice introducing himself, saying he met my mother at Michelle Cordial's wedding and that when she found out that he was moving to Denver, she insisted that he call me.

"Wow," I thought. "Go, Mom, go!" It really gave me such a boost that day.

We agreed to meet at his hotel the next evening. I couldn't have been more shocked by what answered the door. It was the early '80s, mind you, but even then, I could not abide the gold chains that adorned his crispy chest hairs framed by the icky shiny polyester shirt unbuttoned to his navel. Call me particular, but this alarming specimen sported the full ghastly '80's disco look, complete with a wide white belt stretched across his paunch, a pasty white pallor to his skin, topped off with a dramatically receding hairline. He invited me in with that seductive voice of his and said he hoped I didn't mind that he took the liberty of ordering dinner in, and he began to inspire me with chilled champagne. What could my mother have been thinking by giving this bizarre creature her beloved, recently heartbroken daughter's telephone number? It was a syndrome I had seen play out many times before . . . my mother as friend of the friendless. She would take odd ducks under her wing and pump them up good. This time she had gone too far. I narrowly escaped my seducer's clutches that night, and he continued to pursue me with a vengeance until I firmly explained that I had just received a new assignment in Congo, leaving on the next barge, where I planned to live in a convent. I was so utterly disgusted with this dating game. I silently vowed to never swing again.

# Relationships That Dance

*"A good relationship has a pattern like a dance and is built on some of the same rules. The partners do not need to hold on tightly, because they move confidently in the same pattern, intricate but gay and swift and free, like a country dance of Mozart's . . . Now arm in arm, now face to face, now back-to-back—it does not matter which. Because they know they are partners moving to the same rhythm, creating a pattern together, and being invisibly nourished by it."*[*]

—Anne Morrow Lindbergh

I sincerely wish I had read the above morsel of wisdom prior to my actual dating ordeal with Roger. There ought to have been someone standing over me with a stick, rapping my knuckles, forcing me to write that passage over and over again until I owned it, until I got it through my thick head that dating is not supposed to be a form of torture, but in fact something to be enjoyed. In hindsight, I sincerely wish that I could have actually heard the truth in what Roger was trying to say to me when he moved into our building, about his genuine need for his little studio apartment to be his shrine to his independence so that he could recover after he had squandered all his romantic

* Anne Morrow Lindbergh, *Gift from the Sea*, New York: Pantheon Books, 1955, p. 11.

impulses on the wrong gal for the past three years. If I had, I believe I could have been loving and supportive enough to give him what he needed and enjoyed the dance more. Oh well. I suppose he was a psychology major for a reason. I cannot imagine why an intelligent person would not have run for his life and gotten into one of those witness protection/identity change programs upon exposure to me and all my neediness and bizarre ancient issues. Our first little camping trip to Yosemite had been an idyllic romp, and we all vowed to make it a "same-time-next-year" gathering. Upon returning home, Roger had the nerve to ask me out on a "real date" the following weekend.

I freaked out. "Please don't call it a date. I date badly. I turn into a weird pseudo-person even I don't recognize. Trust me, you do *not* want to date me."

If he had asked me to marry him then and there, I probably would have handled it better. We agreed to have a friendly casual dinner together in a little Vietnamese restaurant called Le Bigamist in Haight-Ashbury. It is not there anymore, but the Cha-Cha-Cha is in its place, and it was right down the street from the Persian Zam Zam Room, which had been written up in *TIME* magazine for pouring the perfect martini. The bartender/owner there looked a little like Zero Mostel. He has been there forever and had basically "had it up to here" with all the barhopping punks in the neighborhood. Roger had to coach me on the protocol of the place, to avoid the embarrassment of being thrown out onto the sidewalk, which tended to happen with alarming frequency. The key to actually being served one of those perfect martinis was to slip in quietly, humbly, ideally dressed not too hippie, not too punk, and definitely not too yuppie. The owner was fond of greeting potential customers with a grumbling "There's a bar down the street for people like you," if his razor-sharp antennae picked up on something that rubbed him wrong. He was known to take offense to khakis and Polo shirts as well as long hair and tie-dye. It was random, depending on his mood. You couldn't be in too much of a hurry to be served or you would be ejected for being impatient and rude. We managed to blend in and not offend and enjoyed one perfect martini that night. That small victory, I think, planted a seed in Roger's mind we might actually be perfect for each other.

Now I have probably had no more than a handful of martinis in my entire life. My drink of choice has always been the margarita or the beer. But my ADD brain is urging me to tell this one other martini story right now before I forget. One night as I was swimming upstream trying to keep up with the never-ending needs of our present-day household of two young children, I lost track of the time. I suddenly realized I was late for a meeting I'd promised to attend, and just dashed out the door without explaining any of this to the kids, knowing my husband was there to be on duty for an hour or so. What kind of a meeting created such urgency, you ask? I am so tempted to say a simple PTA meeting or something safe, but I am sensing here that the truth might be funnier, and since I have vowed to lighten up, here goes the truth. I had read in our local newspaper that there was an urgent need for foster parents in our town, and they were holding an informational meeting at the library that night.

Are you laughing yet? It's just that I had really been getting into studying the promises in the Bible and had taken it to heart that through God all things are possible and was really praying for God to use me in a meaningful way. It occurred to me that for some kids, even an inept parent might be better than no parent at all, and I'd really been trying to pay attention to those God whispers in my head, so I figured that when tears came to my eyes reading that story in the paper, it might be a sign that I might need to pay attention. We had just completed a major remodel on our little house and had transformed it into this shingled-Craftsman-style-beyond-our-wildest-dreams-house, thanks to this unbelievable, unexpected inheritance from my extremely humble and thrifty and generous grandparents, and I was wondering how I could give something back. I was only gone for an hour or so, but when I returned home, there was a note on the front door from my always unique eight-year-old daughter with a picture she'd drawn of me holding a martini glass, apparently having a perfectly super time swinging from a tree swing, with this note attached:

> Mommy, I felt like I wanted you tonight. I'm going to bed erly about 8:30 or so. I will say prayers alone and Daddy will tuck me in. Now I learned how to do these

*dwarwings and its fun, so I did one of you! I guess I just lik dwawing these because I thought of you and you're in love with martinies. (I don't know if I spelled that right.) See ya in the morning*

*XOXO Love, Lucy.*

Was I ever glad the social worker for the foster parenting program hadn't accompanied me home! So, this is what she thought I did when I wasn't hanging around the house cleaning, laundering, and cooking! I felt so proud. I keep the note posted in my closet to inspire me to be a little more like that carefree, martini-wielding swinger. In fact, I hope it can be appliqued to my tombstone one day.

---

Would you like to hear the story about the day I finally really knew that Roger loved me? We were all planning to return to Yosemite for the annual camping, hiking, Frisbee-golf fest, when we learned that Roger had a command performance to return to Idaho to do an update on that salmon-trout farming video that had procured all that incredible fish for our infamous first fish fry together shortly after we'd met. The bad news was that it had to happen on our sacred Yosemite weekend. I tried to be big about it, but what I was really thinking was that here is someone who doesn't really care about sacred romantic traditions when there is a chance to chase after big bucks instead. As Rog headed off for the airport, he promised to try to catch up with us.

"Yeah, right," I thought. Anne and I headed up to Yosemite the next day and rendezvoused with all the same gang as last year. It wasn't the same without that Rog. Saturday evening as we were getting ready for dinner, up walked a disheveled Rog, carrying a bouquet of wilted flowers and the biggest salmon-trout you have ever seen as a love offering, looking like someone who had chased a few salmon upstream himself. It turns out that as soon as they finished shooting, he had been able to hop a plane from Boise to San Francisco, then onto a puddle-jumper to Modesto, where he met a guy willing to take him and his large dead fish part of the way to Yosemite. He then hitchhiked several times on up the mountain with people who were somehow not afraid to pick up the tall stranger armed with flowers and a gigantic rapidly thawing fish. I fear these words do not do the moment justice. It was truly a mountaintop experience for me. Here was someone willing to be a total love slave, to be a fool for love, to walk miles in the wrong shoes and leap over tall buildings and fallen giant redwoods for love—all the things I had trained myself to believe existed only in the movies and fairy tales, and he was doing all that to show off for *me*—even though I had been brutally honest with him about all my weird stuff. He blew me away.

Could this be true unconditional love? I was inspired to try to one-up him in the love-slave department, but on me it just seemed icky. I'd leave him mushy love notes, containing things like Matthew Arnold's poem "Dover Beach"*:

> Ah, love, let us be true
> To one another! for the world, which seems
> To lie before us like a world of dreams,
> So various, so beautiful, so new
> Hath really neither joy, nor love, nor light,
> Nor certitude, nor peace, nor help for pain;
> And we are here as on a darkling plain,
> Swept with confused alarms of struggle and fight,
> Where ignorant armies clash by night.

He still doesn't get that one. My worldview was admittedly just a skosh tortured, and his was so simple and upbeat. Somehow, we balanced each other and soldiered on. And darling Anne was there to be an expert witness, urging it all to unfold with giddy delight.

---

* Matthew Arnold, "Dover Beach," Poetry Foundation, https://www.poetryfoundation.org/poems/43588/dover-beach.

# Being Brave

As many of you may have gathered, contrary to predictions, the world did not come to an end on January 1, 2000, Y2K. It was instead a year that began for us with an incredible, thrilling optimism. A few months prior, I had gotten a random call from Anne with the dramatic breaking news that a weird kind of "army guy" was pursuing her. I pictured this big, burly guy who might be more brawn than brains and said I was sure he was harmless and didn't think a thing about it. Anne, by this time, was far more skilled at sabotage tactics than any Army Ranger could ever hope to be, and I was sure she would find a way to outsmart this poor sap. The next thing I knew, she was calling me to confess that she had gone and gotten herself engaged to this army guy, and his name was Gary Kelley, and they were planning a Saint Patrick's Day wedding, and I really needed to meet him. Anne and this Gary were living up in Seattle and were coming down the following weekend.

I still delight in the reality check of our first introduction to the prince who was Gary Kelley. "Weird Army guy" in Anne-speak translates to "dashing Bosnian War Army Ranger/officer/stud muffin and West Point graduate." He was so smart and articulate and quick enough to stay one step ahead of Anne and her clever self-protective devices. He just got her act, big-time. I loved him immediately . . . the way he encouraged Anne to be herself and to wear the lampshade on her head. Anne had always said she would recognize the man she would marry by the way he would rest his hand gently on the small of her back . . . and that was so Gary. They were incredibly tender and natural together. And it was one of the all-time best weddings ever—the Kelley-Murphy Irish-Catholic Saint Patrick's Day 2000 Gala nuptials, complete with flowing Guinness and corned beef and cabbage with all the trimmings. And as much fun as it all was, I still have this vivid memory of Gary looking at his watch a lot and playfully wondering aloud if it might finally be time to whisk his bride off to their honeymoon suite.

At their rehearsal dinner, I said that one of the greatest regrets of my life would always be that I wasn't the one who found Gary and introduced him to Anne, since she had been such a devoted love broker for my husband and me. Anne's toast made a clever allusion to her affinity for the way Moses wandered in the desert for forty years until he reached the Promised Land, having had to wait all these long, lonely years for her true love. Gary had also been wandering in the desert for many years, questioning the meaning of life and love. He had been married very young, and when that marriage failed, he felt distanced from his church when he needed it most. When he met legal eagle Anne, she pointed out that in the eyes of the church, his marriage wasn't really a marriage at all. The church affirmed that with an annulment, so in finding Anne, he was also reconnected with his faith, and they were able to be married in the Catholic Church by her beloved uncle, her dad's brother, Father Larry. I absolutely cherish the memory of talking with Gary at brunch the morning after the wedding. He had this sweet, sentimental, satisfied smile on his face, and he said to me, "I still can't quite believe that I tricked Anne Murphy into marrying me." And then I made him tell me again how he outmaneuvered her every defense.

A few months later, we all met up in Salinas for the fortieth birthday of Anne's darling brother-in-law, Martino. It was also Gary's forty-third birthday and the weekend of our fourteenth wedding anniversary, so there was a lot of celebrating to do. Anne and Gary arrived shortly after we did, looking every bit the blissful young lovers that they were, coming from Mass at the

Carmel Mission. It was a wonderful reunion of all the Yosemite campers of our early courtship. Later, in conversation, I got all messy and sentimental about the news that my dear friend Mary had just been diagnosed with this horrendous terminal lung cancer. They assured me that they would pray for her. A few quick months later, the phone rang with the horrific news that Gary was dead, Thanksgiving weekend 2000, of an unknown heart defect that had managed to survive rigorous army fitness training for war but not a backyard tennis match. Sometimes I still can't quite believe it. The shock of the news flattened me . . . but Anne was just extraordinary. As heartbroken as she was, she refused to miss the fact that God had honored her with sharing in the last incredible, joy-filled years of Gary's beautiful life. Her vision was that every man comes onto this alien planet—a place that sometimes feels so far away from the mother ship where God lives—with a certain fixed number of years on his clock. She marveled that God had used her to connect Gary back with the fullness of his faith and to cap the last years of his precious life with such unmitigated joy. And she later confided that she knew she would love again, because knowing Gary's love finally proved with absolute conviction, once and for always, that she was lovable.

I am amazed by that kind of faith, and I was so inspired to try to grow into that kind of holy wisdom.

Gary's sudden loss so soon after Mary's loss drained me. I didn't sleep for days. I remember trying to go through the motions of being a functioning human being, but I was just such a liability. I was needed to chaperone a bunch of my son's classmates on a marathon field trip, spending the entire day on Angel Island, tracing the experiences of the Japanese American citizens who had been interned there in World War II. I was a shadow of my former self, just lost in that awful fog of grief again. When it was finally time to go home, a very small ferry greeted us for our return trip, because the larger one was being serviced. Unfortunately, it would need to make two trips, meaning my half of the group would remain behind on the island for another half hour or so, just to prolong one of the already longest days of my life. Picture about sixty fifth graders in a circle singing "Ninety-Nine Bottles of Beer on the Wall" for twenty or thirty minutes . . . it had the most dizzying, hypnotic effect on me that I had to lie down on the park bench adjacent to the gangway that led to where the ferry would soon be loading. I fell into a deep daydream that had cleverly incorporated the singing in the background, so that when the ferry arrived and all those kids and teachers traipsed right past me and onto the ferry, in my dreamy in-between state, I could still hear their singing like an earworm in my head, and so I didn't even notice that the island was now in reality perfectly silent, and I was alone . . . except for this nice park ranger jiggling my arm to rustle me into the dreaded reality that I was in fact stranded. He was able to radio the ferry captain that they needed to return for me, and as embarrassing as it was for me having a boatload of ten-year-olds heckling me as they returned, it was nothing compared to what my son endured for weeks afterward. I was greeted with cheers and high fives as I boarded the ferry at last. "Good one, Mrs. Krakow!"

It was a long time before I was invited to shepherd any children again on a field trip. They had to be really desperate to call on the likes of me—which was such a blessing, as I seem to have a complete inability to say the simple word *no* with any degree of conviction.

The year Lucy was eight, I remember talking to her about how amazed I was that she could be so brave when so many beloved people and pets died on her that year—she had attended seven funerals—and that conversation led to her asking me what the bravest thing was I have ever done. I had to admit I honestly couldn't think of a single thing I had ever been brave about. She laughed, because she had seen me being a wimp all the time about snakes in the garden, and sad movies and bloody owies. Later that year when we were house-sitting for some neighbors in the final days before we could move into our newly remodeled house, I'd been cleaning and packing like a maniac, and Lu and her friend Maya had been amusing themselves independently all day. They asked me if I could *please* take them up to the tree swing in the neighborhood for only twenty minutes. I had recently had an epiphany in my Bible study, reading about the Mary and Martha story and so vividly, painfully identifying with the martyr-sister Martha, famous for slaving away in the kitchen and missing the joy of the other sister, Mary, who was wise enough to simply sit at Jesus's feet and bask in the beauty of the moment. I agreed that they had both been so good to let me work that I would take twenty minutes to attempt to be a fun, playful mommy for once during that long, challenging, high-speed, action-packed summer. Our home remodel had gone long as remodels are wont to do, and we had spent the summer trying to buy time by house-sitting. I think we moved four times that summer, and I was duly exhausted.

Maya took the first turn on the swing. We had done this at least twenty times before, but somehow this time, right at the height of the arc, she lost her grip and fell a good fifteen feet down and then rolled another fifteen feet down the hillside until she was stopped by a tree in her path. She was crying hysterically, and I yelled at her not to move until I reached her, thinking she could have broken her neck or her back. I scrambled through the brush and was horrified to see she had actually landed in a wasp's nest in the ground.

All hell broke loose. Maya was being swarmed, and I was being swarmed, and all I could think of was to yell to Lucy to run to the nearby school to call 911. We were both being stung repeatedly in the face, arms, legs, torso, and they were entangled in our hair as we shook our heads trying to fight them off. I was mostly covered by sweats, but poor Maya was dressed in a skimpy sundress and got the worst of it. All we could do was try to run. Thank God, she had survived her fall with only minor scratches and bruises. We stumbled, shrieking down the hill to the school where they tried to soothe us with Benadryl and ice.

An ambulance arrived to take Maya to the emergency room. They asked me if I needed one, too, but I knew there was nothing they could really do for me beyond Benadryl, and I was already so dang uncomfortable that the thought of being in an ambulance and a waiting room was more than I could imagine enduring, so a kind person drove me home, and I drew a bath and tried coping in a suspension of coolish water. My eyes were nearly swollen shut, but I had to call Maya's mother to explain what happened and to tell her how sick and sorry I was about it. She couldn't have been nicer, but it was so painful for me to have had that happen to a child on my watch—to feel so helpless and so insanely out of control. I spent the next few days in bed itching and looking like the Elephant Man . . . frustrated by my thwarted attempt to be fun and playful for a change, and so confused by what it meant for me to crash so badly just trying to "be there" for twenty lousy minutes for the kids. The next day was moving day, and my darling, heroic, capable husband got to do it all by himself.

What was that all about, God? In my blurry Benadryl stupor, I kept hearing the verse "He maketh me to lie down in green pastures . . ." Right! As if that were the only way he could get me to do that? Frighteningly, I'm afraid that might just be the truth. Both my husband and I tend to think we can do anything if we set our minds to it, and we don't have a very healthy attitude about recognizing when we need help. It was really hard for me to ask for help. Those few key days in bed, I found time for a very funny, sweet, intimate dialogue with God. I experienced the pain of it all mercifully kind of remotely and got to sort of set it aside like we do when our bodies go into shock when there really is too much there to be able to feel or fully experience. I railed a little bit with God about the over-the-top Old Testament/plague-of-locusts quality to my personal drama, which really seemed a bit much.

He countered, "Well, you know how much you like a good story."

I got the message that he was dead serious about the need for me to really learn how to *rest* . . . and that if I was too stubborn to do it for myself, he would maketh me lie down . . . because guess what? He is God and I'm not. I also got a clear sense that sometimes that small request for "twenty minutes of fun" really can be the straw that breaks the camel's back and that I need to get better about my boundaries in order to be a better mom/human being/child of God . . . and that I needed to cut back on the giving so much of the time and learn the art of asking for help and to graciously receive it once in a while. And that feeling of being out of control? "Get used to it, babe . . . because I am God and you're most definitely not the one in control." I felt such a sweet surrender to that notion. So many times, in each day when things inevitably get out of control, I just got this mental picture of a little yellow Post-it with God's name on it and slapped it right on whatever issue of the moment was currently frying my circuitry, and it was automatically entrusted into wiser, far more capable hands than my own.

My good friend Renee brought me soup and such comforting tender company and counsel during my enforced bed rest. My children were unbelievably helpful and encouraging and sweet . . . and Lucy even told me she thought I was brave for trying to help Maya. I thought then that being brave wasn't really a quality I felt inspired to explore much further, and I found a new reverence for this rich moment of abundance in my weakness.

Ever since walking beside Mary through her brutal fight for her life, I can't tell you how often the thought "It's not terminal cancer; it's not terminal cancer; I can handle this" loops through my head. I am more grateful for my very manageable yet consistent, daily problems. The minutia doesn't faze me in the same way as it did before. Mary's gift to me is that the lens through which I view the world is forever changed for the positive. She loved to spontaneously blurt out, "Oh, Liz! We are so lucky!" She so loved her life. When she got sick, she was swamped with offers to help. Her aunt insisted they take a trip to visit the holy waters at Lourdes. She was weak, but she clearly needed a miracle, so she ventured to France with her aunt and sisters. Mary seemed dangerously weaker when she returned a week later—the travel had been such a strain—and I was dreading the emotional fallout if she didn't find her miracle. But something wonderful had happened to her spirit there. She told me that when she was fully immersed in the healing waters, it was so icy cold that it became supernaturally warm again . . . and she met our Lord there in a deeply powerful way, so she would never be the same. I was so afraid that she would come back heartbroken and spent, but she experienced an unexpected transformation. So many times, I find myself inserting myself in other people's battles and worry myself to death instead of praying and allowing God to turn my fear into faith. She had boldly risked everything, staking her fate in God's hands, and I think had tasted a bit of life in his kingdom there, where she could begin to imagine what an undistracted life in communion with God might really be like. And she knew for sure it was unspeakably beautiful.

Still . . . it has been so hard to say goodbye to her and to Gary and to Coco. When Mom died, my old friend Chuck sent me a condolence card that I still have that read: "Isn't it wonderful to have loved someone so much that it is so damn hard to say goodbye?" I am indeed most richly blessed. A lot of grief is a small price to pay for getting to have so many people to love.

# Small World

My brother, Andre, married a darling gal, Gwen Jones, from Montana. They met in law school in Colorado and decided to tie the knot in the surreal beauty of Seely Lake, Montana. I was giddy and incredulous that all three of us Koenig kids, in that long, hard decade since losing Mom, had found our one true love. Mom was able to prove she was there that day as well. Our grandparents Ruthie and Phil had been married sixty years ago in nearby Harden, Montana. They were chatting with one of Gwen's guests at the rehearsal dinner, and it turned out he was the doctor who delivered my mom all those years ago.

I was five months pregnant with Lucy at the time, and nearly three-year-old Rog was slated to be the ring bearer. It was the most spectacular setting for a wedding, and the whole weekend was a total joy fest in nature's splendor. The rehearsal had gone well, and we were all set to walk down the aisle, when I noticed young Rog-boy, all dressed up in his navy blazer, looking very sad.

"What's wrong, Rog?"

"I don't want to be the ring *bear*, Mom. I want to be the ring *tiger*!"

And that he was.

# The Boudoir House

When Roger and I found out our second baby was on the way, we decided to put our tiny love shack on the market. We soon had a buyer who gave us ninety days to find a new home. I had looked all over the county, and there was little on the market in our price range that would meet our growing needs. It was early June, and Roger's parents had generously offered us a weekend off to celebrate our five-year anniversary, which also happened to coincide with our friends getting married at the Santa Barbara Music Academy, the very scene of our own matrimonial crime five years ago. We were enjoying the rare luxury of six hours alone together in the quiet of the car, where we could really think and talk and figure out what the heck we were going to do in a month when we were officially homeless. We tried to put our emotions aside—no small feat for *moi*, known to overreact emotionally, even while not under the influence of raging pregnancy hormones. I took out a piece of paper and wrote down our basic wish list: three bedrooms, two baths, level yard, good school district, as close to SF as possible for optimal commuting, good neighborhood ideally near a park, schools, market—all for under $300,000. Optional perks that would be nice: fireplace, hardwood floors, attached garage, and some architectural darlingness.

We looked at the facts in black and white, and I was shocked to realize that we had already seen this house. It had everything we needed, but we remembered vividly how we had run screaming from the house after spending only five minutes in it. We had dubbed it the "Boudoir House." The first thing we noticed when touring it was that its bachelor owner's idea of cleaning was to spray too much Glade air freshener in it, so that you tried to breathe as shallowly as you could as you looked around, to avoid lung damage. The heavy beige drapes were drawn, so it felt very dark. The walls were beige. The carpet was beige. The kitchen was predominantly beige and brown. Just when that became oppressive, the first bathroom assaulted you, painted Pepto-Bismol pink, with the original 1950s pink toilet, tub, and sink. The bedrooms were beige and dark too—that is, until you got to the master bedroom, which was flooded with sunshine so that we could not possibly miss two extraordinarily large photographs of the owner's fiancée, a full-figured gal with ample cleavage spilling forth from a leather teddy topped with a red boa, in one of those awful sultry boudoir photographs that were trendy in the early '90s. It was too much. We ran out of there as if our lives depended on it, before we even found the charming closet-sized master bathroom.

We were incredulous to discover that 100 percent of the items on our wish list added up to the Boudoir House—poetic justice, you might say, after that "cut him off in the boudoir" story I told earlier, which was such a pivotal moment in our early relationship. But how could we seriously consider making an offer on a house that had fully repelled us? I had seen a similar house in the neighborhood go for nearly $75,000 more a few months ago. It had a new kitchen and lots of skylights. I began to think, "What if we lowballed this house?" After all, it had been on the market for six months, scaring people with those photos and all that air freshener. Then we would have the money to purge all that beige and brown stuff, pop in some skylights, air out the Glade, and in a year, we could sell it at a profit and buy a real house! As an additional bonus, we would have a place to live and not have to have our new baby in some seedy motel room. It was a brilliant plan, and since I secretly didn't really even want the house, I became an unusually tough negotiator. I faxed up this borderline insulting offer from our lovely hotel in Santa Barbara—where we were staying as an anniversary gift from Roger's parents—and I told them this was our final offer, take it or leave it because it was our anniversary, and I didn't want to fritter it away by the fax machine.

They took it! We didn't know whether to celebrate or freak out. We closed escrow in less than a month and arrived in our new neighborhood the day of its annual Fourth of July gala in the tiny park across the street from our new home. The entire street was blocked off from through traffic by a line of Weber grills. There were tons of kids making a parade with makeshift instruments. We were warmly greeted by Marty next door, who informed us that his wife was also expecting a baby. And that's when I met wonderful Mary, who delivered a baby girl named Sarah just nine weeks after we had Lucy. Both mothers and daughters became the best of friends, and we put down roots in that neighborhood like I never thought possible.

I realized I had been a snob and an idiot to think I knew anything at all about what makes a house a home, and I soon quit the real estate racket. We were a community, in the realest, corniest sense of the word. We looked out for each other, drinking margaritas together at sunset and picking groceries up for each other whenever we were doing a run to the market. We didn't hesitate to borrow an egg or a cup of sugar whenever we needed anything. There was always plenty of tea and sympathy and solidarity. We would meet in the street with our dogs and a cup of coffee to start each day. We even had an emergency room doctor in the neighborhood who was willing to treat children needing stitches or suffering a dislocated elbow and give expert tourniquet advice.

And just around the corner was this sleepy little church that loved children and their parents who thought they were going to church for their kids' sake or were hungering for that one quiet contemplative hour per week to experience life with no interruptions. Mary told me about it, saying that if she weren't Catholic, that was the church she would go to. And if that wasn't enough, Connie, my best friend from my real estate office, told me her husband, Dodge, was one of the Sunday School teachers, and the kids adored him immediately and began to insist on going to "Dodge's Church." When I stood in the street where Mary and I had met not so long ago, and again seven years later to sob in each other's arms over the news that she had cancer and there was absolutely nothing they could do, I felt so old and alone. But I had a place to go with my sadness, that reminded me I could never be truly alone.

The church was a heroic place that saved lives all the time. It was a grace-filled place that sent money from their Grace Fund to families who get horrible news like Mary's family did, even though they were not even members of the church. It was a place full of prayer warriors who believed in miracles, and love and the transforming power of the Holy Spirit. It was a teaching church that poured out real-life skills each week to help folks stare down the life-draining values of this world and open our imaginations to see that through God all things are possible, and that we can do all things through Christ, who strengthens us. It was a place where people grew, just by the simple act of showing up with a willingness to explore and receive. Just baby steps, one foot in front of the other. It reminded us of the radical truth that we cannot possibly earn our way to God, that it is a truly free gift, meant to liberate us from the slavery of trying to get it all done under our own power. It was a place to experience real peace and to rest in this truth: "Come to me all you who are weary and burdened and I will give you rest. Take my yoke upon you and learn from me, for I am gentle and humble in heart, and you will find rest for your souls. For my yoke is easy and my burden is light" (Matthew 11:28–30). It was a place that encouraged us to dwell on hope and all good things and to forgive ourselves and others by the power of Christ's passionate, extravagant love and his supreme sacrifice on the cross. It was a place that filled us up with joy and challenged each individual to discover her/his potential. It was a place where we met a God who loves us like the perfect parent, who made us to be a part of an extended family, with a purpose that filled our hearts to overflowing . . . where we learned to count our abundant blessings and no longer feel the need to keep a record of wrongs. It was a place that mourned with you and celebrated the ultimate healing and reward of a loved one being welcomed into heaven.

*We will grieve not, rather find strength in what remains behind.*
—William Wordsworth

Flashing back to September 11, 2001, when a disaster of unfathomable magnitude rocked the world . . . I don't know if I dare admit this, but I think it didn't quite register on the Richter scale for me the way it did for most people. It was shocking and devastating, but I felt sort of a quiet surrender to the horror of it. When Roger got home from work that night, we didn't talk much but also didn't know what to do with ourselves, so we sort of numbly walked holding hands to our little Hillside Church. There were about forty people spontaneously gathered there, and we all just prayed for an hour or so. There was an eerie calm in it, knowing we were alive to wait on God and witness him pull good from this sickening wreckage.

Is it possible to be pre-disastered? I think our family was already in shock from the news just the week before, when Lucy's sweet eight-year-old classmate Carolyn was swept out to sea and drowned by a rogue wave while spending the last day of summer at the beach that she loved. Two months before that, my friend and writing partner Katie lost her fiancé, Pat, in a freak accident with a train. Three months earlier, my precious next-door-neighbor-and-first call-for-help, Mary, nonsmoking mother of three, lost her battle with lung cancer. The month before that, we buried my grandpa, my mom's dad, at ninety. I remember it had really struck me that day that it was actually possible to live to a ripe old age . . . it seemed so long since we'd gotten to celebrate a fully lived life at a funeral. Then the incredible Mary Cook slipped away, one of the founding members of our church; she wasn't much taller than my eight-year-old but had faithfully reflected the mighty face of God through the boundless kindness in her deep-brown baby-harp-seal eyes for the past ninety-three years. And then my cousin Jim, who had spent most of his life in a wheelchair, paralyzed in a car accident shortly after he and my cousin Susie had their first baby. Four times that year we heard the haunting hymn "On Eagles' Wings":

> And He will raise you up on eagle's wings
> Bear you on the break of dawn
> Make you to shine like the sun
> And hold you in the palm of His hand.

And the "annus horribilis," as Queen Elizabeth would say, ended that Sunday following Thanksgiving, as we learned that Anne's shiny, precious triathlete of a new husband, married only eight months, had died at age forty-three of a heart attack on the tennis court, surrounded by family in her parents' backyard. We had just spent the weekend before with them, basking in the radiant miracle of their love story, spending just enough time for our children to fall in love with Uncle Gary. I fell on my face that night after the kids were asleep, right there on the fluffy carpet in Lucy's room and just sobbed and prayed for answers. Why Anne and Gary? Why not me? I could die tomorrow and honestly feel I'd had a full life! And the quiet voice said, "So why are you still acting like you are in prison?"

My mind jumped to the story Earl Palmer, pastor of the church I attended at Cal, once told, drawing the analogy of a kite as the ultimate symbol of perfect freedom. But it can only fly when it is tethered to something solid . . . just like we can only be perfectly free to fly when we hold on to God's really long arms. For me it was more like free-falling from an airplane that year, but the fear I'd felt all my life had dramatically receded. I was just too burnt out to feel it anymore. I never even thought about going splat at the end of the fall because I just thought about God all the time, and I knew he would catch me if my parachute failed to open. I heard the familiar quiet voice in my head saying, "You think you've got a patent on pain? Look around you." (Note: God normally doesn't speak in this tone, but I've found that he is supremely able to speak in a unique way that each individual can understand . . . gentle sarcasm seems to work best for me.) It had been almost too much to bear the secondhand pain I witnessed all around me. This wasn't even about me; the real story was the people who had taken the direct hits and the grace that seemed to enfold them.

From the hideous debris of 9/11 rose stories of such courage and character, they just stopped the whole world in its tracks. And as Anne said goodbye to her darling Gary, she prayed, "Thy will be done." And as Mary battled cancer, she had never walked closer to God. And as Katie coped with the loss of her precious fiancé, we dared each other to write about our baggage and to hold each other accountable. As I watched their stories play out, I thought, "I have got to try to get that kind of faith going in my life."

C. S. Lewis wrote: "Pain is God's megaphone to awaken a deaf world." Dear God, please tell me all these people didn't have to die because I was asleep at the wheel and needed to be awakened to shed my scaly old self and come fully alive.

"Life is about joy and sorrow. We share in both the crucifixion and the resurrection of Christ," to quote our pastor Prince Altom, who had just lost the daddy he adored.

I began to thank God with a new earnestness for my petty run-ins with the police, and for forever trying to get my house clean and being so dog-tired all the time. I knew I would never be able to make sense of any of this, but I had the hope that comes from knowing God will make something good come from all the suffering that seemed to be running rampant in the world, and that hope is enough. It takes me out of the driver's seat where I am so dangerous and elevates God to his rightful place.

Later I watched the evening news report that we were now officially at war with Iraq, and I felt the silent scream well up inside me and wanted to howl with dread. I couldn't really sleep, but sleepless nights are some of my best visits with God because he is incredibly always up for conversations at any hour, and he is the world's best listener and the cheapest therapist, and I would have sworn he audibly said, "Why don't you just get up and write about it if you're so worked up?" And so I rolled over in bed and saw underneath the door that he'd even left the light on for me.

Over the years I have tried to live by those words from Ephesians 6:11, "Put on the full armor of God," asking him to go before me as I go into battle . . . this day and every day. And instead of the wild tornado I was so used to living in, I could go to my free-fall mode, where I could enjoy the sacred moments as well as feel the adrenaline of the adventure as it rushed past and also see God in his grace going before me, commanding the elements, directing my path—a path so lovingly crafted just for me, that consists of not one single thing more than I can handle.

I love what the grandma said at the end of the movie *Parenthood*: "Some people like the merry-go-round . . . me, I've always liked the roller coaster." The roller coaster is a great metaphor for life: full of highs and lows, anticipation and thrills, courage and terror and passion—always an adventure, always evolving—as opposed to that hypnotic, mind-numbing, hamster wheel safety of the merry-go-round.

I found this prayer among my mom's letters as I was searching for clues and answers in her desk after she died, and I've kept it with me ever since.

### Answered Prayer

I asked God for strength, that I might achieve,
I was made weak, that I might learn humbly to obey . . .
I asked God for health that I might do greater things,
I was given infirmity that I might do better things . . .
I asked for riches, that I might be happy,
I was given poverty that I might be wise . . .
I asked for power that I might have the praise of men,
I was given weakness that I might feel the need of God . . .
I asked for all things that I might enjoy life,
I was given life that I might enjoy all things.
I got nothing that I asked for but everything I had hoped for.
Almost despite myself, my unspoken prayers were answered.
I am among all men most richly blessed.

—Unknown Soldier

# Dog Spelled Backward

Freckles was our first baby, helping us to establish our sense of family as soon as we returned from our honeymoon in Yugoslavia and Italy. We got her one sad, vulnerable day when we were home trying to process the devastating news that our dear friend Coco had died in a freak car accident. *AM San Francisco* was on TV for distraction. They were doing a segment on how to brush your dog's teeth, and Freckles was their humiliated model. We decided: "We have *got* to go save Freckles for Coco!" It felt somehow redemptive to impulsively adopt her. She gave us our first inkling of what it would be like to actually be parents, by attempting to take care of her. Looking back at how many times we lost her and how many times we had to bail her out of the pound, I think we perhaps should have given more thought to our fitness for parenting. She was crafty; it was always a challenge to keep her fenced in to our yard. And she was fond of stowing away in my car so she could surf her golden beagle ears out the window as I drove. Once when I stopped for gas, she slipped out without me seeing, and I drove off, only to see her in my rearview mirror galloping behind me as I accelerated down the road.

I remember when I was very pregnant with our first human baby, I got a call from a woman who had been riding her horse near the Marin watershed and had found our dog bleeding in a creek bed. It appeared she had been shot. She had called the Humane Society first, and they had taken Freckles to a nearby animal hospital. It turned out that Freckles had been chasing a deer, and a brave forest ranger had shot our small, very nonthreatening domestic mutt to protect the deer that have so overpopulated our mountain that they have to survive by eating everything I have ever attempted to plant in our garden every night. The pregnancy hormones were surging as I called my husband at work sobbing and choked out the tabloidesque news, "Freckles has been shot!" He attempted to talk me down out of my tree, saying he was with a client and that I needed to try to handle this myself. I raced to the vet to find Freckles alive but with a bullet lodged inoperably near her heart.

In hindsight, the experience mellowed her considerably in that special way God has of growing good things out of tragedy. She slowed down and became the greatest nanny to our kids. Once my daughter, Lucy, gave us the slip when she was a toddler, during a neighborhood party in the front yard, and Freckles's wagging tail was like a beacon as we looked up the hill around the corner and located Lu blissfully digging in a neighbor's garden a few houses away.

By the time Freckles died, she was blind and deaf and fifteen years old. It came at the end of a long streak of losses in Lucy's young life—first Grammy; then Gramps; then Uncle Gary and Mary, her second mother next door; then Mary Cook, her ninety-three-year-old best buddy at church; then, incredibly, her precious second-grade classmate Carolyn was swept out to sea by a rogue wave all in the same year—and she wasn't taking it too well. None of us had the skills to process that tsunami. I think Lucy stepped up and spoke at three of those funerals.

"Sometimes it seems like everyone I know is dead," she said, so world weary at eight.

We mourned Freckles for a good six months or so. One day in early December, I was running Lu to a 12:00 surprise birthday party, only to learn when we arrived that I had misread the invitation (*moi?*), and it was supposed to start at 2:00. So we decided to hit the nearby mall to do a little Christmas shopping. We were immediately detoured by the Humane Society's display in the center of the mall. There was a beautiful petite Alaskan husky/shepherd mix in the pen. Her paws were crossed delicately one over the other, and her soulful eyes appeared to be sort of rolled up heavenward, as if to say, "This circus is *so* beneath my dignity." Her name was Sky, and she indeed seemed to be heaven sent. She was ten years old, and her family had moved and couldn't take her. She was reluctant to respond to us; she was so embarrassed and depressed. She broke our hearts. We would have impulsively taken her right home with us, but they wanted to watch her because she had been throwing up earlier in the day, probably because she was so deep and emotional, trying to cope with her abandonment. And we thought we ought to include our other two family members in the idea. I assumed the kids had their hearts set on a puppy, but Lu insisted passionately that Sky was the only dog she could ever love.

The next day we went back to visit at the animal shelter, and everyone fell in love with shy Sky. We were relieved to hear a few days later that she seemed strong and healthy and adoptable. My biggest fear was her age, since I'd been feeling so weary of drama and grief, but we took a leap of faith together, and truly Sky blossomed like a fresh puppy. And in so many ways she was like the literal manifestation of the eyes of God in our household . . . in her eyes were a longing and ancient intelligence and a bottomless pool of unconditional love. She delighted in the simple things—just being together, taking hikes—and the look on her face was so wounded and worried when voices got raised in anger, it just stopped us right there in our tracks and defused the tension and made us laugh. She was so sensitive that she gave us all a heightened awareness of not doing anything that might horrify the dog. It is so poetic that the word dog is *God* spelled backward . . . it is so like God to do things in an unexpected backward way to get our attention. She is now a fixture at church on Sunday mornings, an official greeter tethered outside to welcome people. I know of one elderly lady who comes only for the music and to visit with Sky on Sundays, so Sky is clearly on her own little mission from God. I have even taken to including her at our Thursday morning Bible studies because of her innate ability to comfort and encourage people. It is uncanny to watch her antennae perk up when someone is in distress and in need of a warm fuzzy.

Walking the Sky-dog was a sacred ritual, each morning and each evening.

And I dragged her on my rounds in between, because I knew our days together were numbered and she had so much more to teach me. She showed me so poetically and gracefully how it is to walk with God. When I'd lag, she'd prance back and engage me. When I was weary and needed to sit down and breathe in a little nature, she'd agree that was a very good thing, too, and together we'd ponder our existence. When it was a dreary morning, and I maybe didn't feel like walking, she'd encourage me like the most obnoxious physical trainer: "Come on . . . it'll be fun . . . I dare you . . . just give it a try!" And she'd do this comical prancy-dancy thing that was so full of contagious energy and enthusiasm, it launched my day and got me moving. I was so hoping that in the way God's timetable is not our own, she would have been with us for a long time more.

Alas, we had to put sweet Sky to sleep June 19, 2008, at nearly seventeen years old. She started failing the week that we celebrated twenty years of marriage and our firstborn son, Roger, graduated from high school and then shipped out to Europe for a month. She was stoic and noble as she faded away in our much emptier nest. She taught me a few more lessons about patience and courage and faith in the end. We will always love her and miss her. The best thing you can say when you lose someone you love is that they left the world a better place because they were here. The challenge is to hold on to the good and delight-filled memories that came from their years on this lonely planet and not get stuck dwelling on the sadness.

One of my oldest and favorite dog stories is about Annie, from my teen years. Orphan Annie, another pound treasure, was a radiant Australian shepherd mix whose platinum tresses would have been the envy of any Hollywood starlet. Mom had picked out the little fluff ball from the pound in a weak moment following the unexpected demise of Rufus, who had collapsed in a diabetic coma from too many stolen boxes of See's Candy and freshly baked cookies sneaked from the counter. Rufus was a dog of very little brain who carried a large rock in his mouth everywhere he went and would drop it in the toilet when he went to drink. Mom's act of mercy sealed Annie's fiduciary loyalty to her forever. They went everywhere together. When Mom died suddenly from a massive heart attack, no one thought to explain her absence to the dog. After a month or so, Annie just disappeared. I had just quit my job in Colorado and moved home with Dad to sort things out and wrangle this surreal new rudderless weight of sadness.

After Annie had been missing a few days, we were lucky enough to find her curled up in a muddy embankment under the dock behind our house, weak and shivering. She just seemed to be wanting to die and catch up to wherever it was that Mom had gone.

We had her evaluated by the vet, who said he could find nothing wrong with her except that she had quit eating. We opted to put her on intravenous feeding and fluids for a few days to see if she could regain some strength, because the thought of losing her, too, just wasn't an option. I visited her in her kennel daily and just talked to her and petted her and cried about her and Mom. Slowly she began to come back, and we bonded in our shared grief therapy. I think we both felt understood and a little less lonely. I still marvel at the depth of her loyalty and her deeply felt loss. She bounced back and was with me for many years, a kind of extension of my mom, who walked me through the spinster years before I met my husband, had babies, and could begin to fathom a new definition of home. There she was in the wedding photos, perfect, smiling, and radiant in every pose . . . and again at the patio barbecue when we brought baby Roger home from the hospital. Mom should have been there, but there was Annie reminding us that she was . . . just in a different dimension.

I happened to be home for a visit at Dad's when it was Annie's time to die, following a well-loved, fully lived life . . . the life I would have wished for my mom. I got to sit up with Annie all night, knowing this was it. I was grateful to get to hold her and comfort her, but I was too spineless to do that awful trip to the vet for the final goodbye, so Dad did it alone. Just like he did all the funeral arrangements alone for Mom . . . and in the blurry storm of his grief, he inadvertently chose a charming plot with a view of the nearby gas station, which I regrettably pointed out to him in my self-absorbed frustration. In hindsight, I realized it is the exact spot my self-mocking mom used to point to as the place she would someday be buried, where we could "race past in our cars and wave and toss our beer cans at her" from the freeway overpass.

The best thing you can say when you lose someone you love is that they left the world a better place because they were here, and the challenge is to hold on to all the good and delight-filled memories and avoid clinging to the discouraging notion that the world suddenly seems a lot duller without them in it.

# Going Crazy in the Great Outdoors

Camping has always been a delightful way for families to get down and dirty and commune with nature. The kids love to get dirty and run wild, and the parents can enjoy a respite from housecleaning and the simple pleasure of opening a can of Dinty Moore Stew and calling it dinner, followed by the added thrill of s'mores over the open campfire. It is the only time I ever heard a note of heartfelt appreciation for my culinary skills from my children. It had been a long, challenging summer, so when my friend Danielle called to invite us to share her large campsite at Samuel P. Taylor campgrounds near the coast about forty minutes away, I jumped at the chance. Danielle is a single mom, and our sons are buddies. She had invited us with ulterior motives, because when she arrived at her designated campsite, she learned that she had been assigned a remote horse-camping outpost, which was so far removed from civilization, it kind of gave her the creeps to be there alone with her two boys. We could drive in with our gear, but the road was closed to any other traffic. We all camped there happily for two nights. It was almost close enough for my husband to commute to San Francisco, but when Monday morning came, he said he had to work late and would probably not make it back to sleep that last night. No problem. We were fearless, established pioneer women.

That night we were gathered around the lanterns at the picnic table playing cards with the kids, and up the road walked the first humans we had seen in days. Four large men holding beer cans walked past our campsite wordlessly and headed up the trail. It seemed like a strange time to be going for a hike, with only a flashlight to guide them. My antennae went on alert status, and when their large bodies looped back down the hill about a half hour later, there were only two of them. The drama queen in me jumped to the conclusion that we were being surrounded, and that something awful was about to happen. I was having flashbacks to *Deliverance* and the *Texas Chainsaw Massacre*—movies I knew better than to actually see, but I was still haunted by what I'd heard about them. I was successfully able to impose my hysteria on Danielle, and soon the only intelligent (!) thing to do was to strike camp and head for the safety of home an hour away. I just knew I wouldn't get a minute of sleep all night long trapped in a tent with my overreactive, alarmist imagination. It was pitch dark, around 9:00 p.m. Mysterious things were already rustling the bushes with hateful glee. I had to move fast, heroically, to protect my cubs—and I do not have a courageous bone in my entire body. It is truly pathetic.

I trained the headlights of my car onto the campsite as we all flew into action to pack up. The entire process couldn't have taken more than twenty minutes, and there was barely room to wedge two children into seat belts in between unrolled sleeping bags, ice chests, dogs, and laundry . . . both cars were packed to the gills. I squeezed into the car to make our escape and found to my delight that I had run the battery dead. The jumper cables, if either of us had them, were buried deep beneath all our stuff, and we couldn't swear we had them at all. The only thing we could do was to pile everyone into Danielle's car and throw ourselves on the park ranger's mercy a few miles away. He thought we were certifiable loons but took pity on us and followed us back up the mountain with his jumper cables, and by midnight we were off to freedom and our warm, fluffy beds waiting at home, alive to greet another day. For some of us, too much nature and fresh air can be absolutely toxic.

# MOM: Upside Down, Inside Out, and Backward = WOW

My new excuse for not writing much lately was simply this: Life has not been very funny. This was eloquently confirmed for me by my wise-beyond-her-thirteen-years-old daughter, Lucy, one night. We were all in the kitchen, and I was flinging together something we would gamely call dinner. Sixteen-year-old Rog grabbed the top of a hot skillet with his bare hands and shrieked as the steaming hot lid clanged to the floor. We shoved his hot pink hand into a bowl of ice water, but it appeared to be just one of those things that he wasn't going to be ready, willing, or able to rebound from any time soon. He had sort of had it after a week of conferences with teachers and the principal and groundings triggered by a special little run-in with the juvenile authorities. It seemed as if the hot skillet was an apt metaphor for his recent new life of living dangerously in the proverbial frying pan fire, and he allowed it all to cascade around him in that moment and writhed on the floor in agony for an extended period of time.

Lucy took pity on him and began to tenderly apply some of the wacky home remedies that she'd become so fond of since her recent success in nuking her pesky, persistent plantar wart by sleeping with banana peels taped to her feet at night. (Give a shout-out to internet wisdom!) First, she wrapped his throbbing thumb in a banana peel and secured it with tape. Then she tried slopping on some aloe and surrounded it with aluminum foil on the next finger. Then ice cubes and plastic wrap and foil on another finger. My gigantic little boy was feeling so pathetic he let this all go on until he looked very much like the foil robot boy of his seven-year-old Halloween costume. I turned around from cooking dinner and took all this in and just burst into gut-wrenching laughter that was indeed so pent up, so foreign that tears were mixed in there as well. My daughter just stared at me and said, "Mom, I haven't seen you laugh like that in a long time."

Wow.

It scared the heck out of me. She was right. And my mind instantly leaped to a memory of my mom telling me wistfully that my dad used to think she was funny but not anymore, as they approached their twenty-fifth anniversary. That was the year my dad shut down and moved, temporarily, he thought, into a quiet studio apartment in his little midlife crisis . . . and within a few months, Mom died from an imploding heart. I resolved right there in the kitchen to somehow find a way to laugh more, as if my life depended on it—because I know for certain that it does.

I was a terrible math student. I still remember vividly how even in twelfth grade, everyone else's favorite math teacher could make me cry in frustration because I was so lost. I could never track with mathematical logic, but numbers do hold an abstract fascination for me. They help me to remember and mark and notice things . . . patterns, anniversaries. Not in any woo-woo numerology/astrology/feng shui/voodoo context, but just as markers that somehow give me pause in my brain wiring, stopping me in my tracks, causing me to remember, to note that something *bigger* than moi (!) just may be operational here. In his always inspired, creative, mysterious way, God has me paying attention to the finer details in the way he has so faithfully and surely laid out his plans of rescuing my life from the train wreck it would certainly be with me at the helm.

As I began to write this, I glanced at the clock on the top of my screen, and it was 11:11a.m., reminding me we were married on June 11. When I met my darling husband in our apartment building in San Francisco, the address was *2266*. Our first home, the Love Shack, was *22* Hillside in San Anselmo; our second home was *66* El Camino, which means "the road." And God cleverly placed Hillside Church (reminding us of our first home address) right down the road where we could practically trip over it, to make sure our spiritual growth was so lovingly nurtured. The pastor there once dared us to wake up to wonder, asking how often we experience the WOW moments in our daily lives . . . not nearly enough, Mrs. Crankypants had to admit. It is worth noting that there are *sixty-six* valentine-from-God books/love letters full of wisdom in his bestselling book, the Bible, and around that time I got to see with my own misty eyes, our 44th president of the United States, Barack Hussein Obama, inaugurated president, and I felt like my heart was full to overflowing with joy and hope and optimism for a change. All those matching double-digits, divisible by eleven, emblems of symmetry, stability, marking our path and pointing the way. I was renewed, inspired.

Wowed.

A few years ago, I sat on a jury as the thirteenth juror in a road rage case. The number thirteen is an unlucky number for a reason. It means you must sit there and listen and be available if needed but are not allowed to weigh in with *any* (no, not a single one!) of your passionate, heartfelt opinions, which is pretty much my definition of hell. If you must know, my opinion was that there can only be road rage when one idiot takes the bait of another idiot, and together, they tango until one of the idiots' fancy fast cars gets banged up, and because people generally do not take responsibility for their bad selves anymore in our culture, they sue each other. And I mean that in the kindest, most nonjudgmental way. To mete out justice, the jury deliberated for three days, inconveniencing not only me, but an emergency room doctor, a teacher, a social worker, a counselor . . . people who could be out there saving lives! Instead, we were sitting on this ridiculous jury, at great public expense, deciding the (obvious, to me) fate of two latent juvenile delinquents amped up on testosterone. Once the deliberations were complete, I was unceremoniously dismissed, without even the satisfaction of hearing the judge's ultimate ruling. I was undone. To this day, I remain very jaded and cynical about what constitutes justice in our legal system. It was so much grandstanding, so much ado about nothing, it reminded me of *The Jerry Springer Show*. Don't get me started.

Incredibly, the jury pool chucked up my name again. Could it really have been eighteen months ago, so I was eligible *again*? I had many fun moments with myself pondering what I would say when asked if there was any reason I could not serve as a juror this time. Finally, I decided that I could convincingly say that I have *very* strong opinions on the best of days and that I might have a teensy bit of a bad attitude hanging over from my recent thirteenth juror experience.

It ultimately turned out that the judge was looking for a three-week commitment to be on an indictment grand jury, and as I lamely pitched my prefabbed excuse-spiel, the judge leveled a disarming gaze at me and said, "We really need smart people on this jury . . . and I think you will find it an exciting and rewarding experience." Dang. I am a sucker for that kind of flattery. He had me. It ultimately gave me a wild ride of a story. Unfortunately, I believe I signed things that agreed they could send me up the river, tarred and feathered for life, if I dare discuss them until the case resolves.

I was again overcome in a seemingly innocuous moment, which I should really refer to as my own private road rage moment. I was late on one of my hamster-wheel chauffeur loops, stuck in traffic behind the lamest of all bumper stickers: "God couldn't be everywhere, so He invented mothers." There is a very desperate epidemic of hovering, helicoptering parents who actually believe that sentiment, and it is draining the life out of them. I mentally edited the thing to read: "Mothers cannot be everywhere; that's why they need God."

Wow.

My road-ragin' mind raced back to that recent Wow-sermon, and in one reverse-dyslexic leap turned the word upside down to read *Mom*. In that quirky moment, God showed me it is all connected in that upside-down, inside-out and backward way. There he goes again, speaking to me in a language even (perhaps only?) I can understand. Being a mom is chock full of mind-blowing WOW moments. It is just a constant challenge to keep showing up with those God-flavored glasses on (where did I see them last?), so I can see the truth and beauty and wow in the fairly consistent onslaught of agonizing moments of fear and heartache and lameness that is also the definition of being a mom—especially of teenagers.

My son had been on a crime spree. In two and a half months of being a legal driver, his size 13 (there's that number again!) feet on the tiny little gas pedal had earned him no fewer than five citations and his own day in court in which the judge impounded his license, fined him $1,000, and very publicly told him he was clearly a terrible driver. I had been trying to tell him that very thing in a kinder, less expensive way, but sometime teenage boys have to hear it from a higher authority. The upside of this was a sweet humbling and an awakening to a much-improved work ethic in school; a new twenty-two-hour-a-week job at the café near our house, which helped him pay his court fines in one month; and an adorable new girlfriend (who is an excellent driver!).

I must brag that I conspiratorially pointed her adorableness out to him one day, saying, "I totally noticed Christine checking you out at the recent music department concert, and I really think it's important for you to think about hanging more with the gals for a fresh new perspective."

Best of all, I successfully held my tongue when I was tempted to make the connection between how hanging out with the guys so much appeared to me to be directly connected with poor decision-making and his costly recent crime spree! Much to my giddy delight, instead of repelling him, I actually got him to listen! Oh, I must say, my joy runneth over! So then a tennis buddy of mine shared this exciting new factoid: Most girls these days are on the pill to keep acne under control, so now they all think they are bulletproof. I am so weary from the constant battle.

The warfare mentality is so alien to most women, but it is naive to disregard the very real threat. The truth is you *do* have to fight for your life . . .

children . . . marriage. And more than anything, I had to fight for my attitude to gravitate upward toward all the good, all the blessings that kept getting tangled up in all the muck. Every day was like a giant Easter egg hunt, looking for the beauty, the perfect moments that might come disguised as something ordinary—or even smelly like a rotten egg. I was so exquisitely capable of missing the sacredness of this moment as I busied myself worrying about the future or flogging myself for some misspent moment in the past.

I've got to be honest here. The dark cloud that I had been processing that year, my forty-eighth—the year that killed my mother—the memory that came rushing in around me as I lingered behind that irritating bumper sticker was a little thing no one wants to talk about, but it happened . . . right here in the glorious shadow of the Golden Gate Bridge. On the day before school started for her four teenagers, a precious, spunky mother that I liked and played tennis with jumped over the rails of that gorgeous bridge into the sea to her death. No one saw it coming. She was a cute, feisty, fit, busy, and proud mother. Sure, her marriage was in a hole, but I do not know many marriages that really thrive when the children are in the teen years. She seemed to have it all together but was apparently the loneliest person on the planet. The last time I saw her in one of our mom loops, she asked me if I was going to be coaching the high school tennis team the following year because she hoped her son was going to play. The last time the two of us played tennis, it was in a competitive match for my team, and she almost beat me, and I wish I had been more about friendliness and less about winning that day. She could have used a win.

At her funeral I sat with my dear friends and tennis coaches, Ed and Eileen, who have been married more than fifty years, managing to raise six incredible boys and several foster sons. They are two of the most positive, loving people you will ever meet. Ed was just distraught, saying he had just seen her the day before, running by the tennis courts with a smile and a wave. In the tears that he shed that day, I know he, too, was wondering if he had missed an opportunity to let her know she was seen and loved and valued. She was a highly competent, organized, very giving woman, known by everyone it seemed . . . but her true needs and sweet desires of her heart were missed by all. On her dark night of the soul, she chose not to reach out for help and expose her vulnerability—and I really fear that happening again to someone I know and love.

I see so many women today operating on such slim margins, carrying too much of the weight of the world on their puny human shoulders. I call it "the curse of the competent woman." We all need to get better at asking each other, and God, for help. We need the wisdom to reframe our challenges as annoying but necessary messengers of needed growth, as secret change agents. Menopause mandates that we change, so *heads up, gals*!

My precious neighbor and sister-of-the-heart Barb told me the basic lesson menopause teaches is that our multitasking days are over. We need to make the shift to focusing on one thing at a time, with a quieter mind, with reverence. The shallow, tap-dancing-as-fast-as-we-can-hormone that is designed to help us stay one step ahead of toddlers is spent *(hallelujah!)* and no longer needed. What is needed now goes much deeper because we are deeper. Shallowness does not satisfy us anymore. We humans tend to resist change by nature, but we must hold on and actively welcome the inevitable changes that come in life—because let's face it: We would all be bored to tears if things just stayed the same all the time. Jesus himself built the whole message in his life story on the fact that pain and brokenness is where real power and promise and hope begin when he laid down his life as a ransom for all mankind to have free access to his gift of amazing grace.

We need to pump each other up *every chance we get* . . . err on the side of love. Daggers in the heart are inevitable this side of paradise and knowing that is half the battle. I am praying for that family to be so gently cradled by God throughout the rest of their lives for having faced this nightmare. And I am hoping that her story will inspire us survivors to be a little less stingy with the kind words to the people in our lives.

Time and time again, if I am going through a storm or a valley, if I can just keep showing up, daring God to show me the beauty in the wreckage, he is faithful to do so. My daily mantra has become "Never give up, never give up." It can't be an option.

I once got to spend the week of my birthday and the Fourth of July in an un-air-conditioned Reno dorm room chaperoning twelve thirteen- and fourteen-year-old volleyball players, to whom I was invisible at best, an annoyance/embarrassment at worst. By the end of the first day, I had lost my voice and developed a nasty cough and sinus condition and a fever, which was difficult to even diagnose in the 106-degree weather. There had been a serious fire around Lake Tahoe that week, burning thousands of acres, so the air quality was at an all-time low; combining with the high altitude, it had the effect of drying out my eyeballs, nostrils, and throat so that I felt like I was swallowing razor blades. By the end of the second night of playing volleyball, it was going on 10:30 p.m., and we still hadn't eaten dinner. I was quietly amusing myself there courtside, with fantasies of a swift, merciful death, literally wishing to be anywhere but here.

Moments later, an attractive older couple, who turned out to be organizers of this *gigantic* festival of ten thousand girls from all over the world, approached me, asking me if this was the Absolute 14s team. I said it was, and then they asked if this was Lucy Krakow's team, and I said it was, and I croaked out the factoid that I was her mother . . . and they smiled and told me Lucy was a very special young lady, and they wanted to meet her. She had entered an essay contest—"What This Volleyball Festival Means to Me"—and had apparently won the whole thing. They went on to say her essay had moved them to tears, and that they had been certain that Lucy was sixteen or seventeen years old and were stunned to learn she was only thirteen. They waited for the game to finish and approached Lu to congratulate her and give her a hug, and in that moment, I realized that I would not have wanted to be anywhere but right there, right then. It would have been such a loss to have missed seeing that sweet triumph for my girl who had taken such a beating that long season, riding the bench more than any other player, so gratefully I watched this valentine-from-God moment play out, with my very own parched, cranky, grumbly eyes, as God elevated her spirit so perfectly.

It was such a vivid illustration for me that life really is often darkest just before the dawn . . . that pain arrives like a messenger to kick us in the rear and get our attention . . . and just when we embrace it, the bomb is dismantled, and the dawn can come.

I had to laugh at the backstory to this proud moment. I had one night in a lovely hotel with my friend Debbie to refresh me before my chaperoning duty was to begin. We'd had a nice dinner and a giant margarita when I got a panicked phone call from my daughter, who had just finished dinner at 11:00 p.m. and realized her story deadline was the following morning at 11:00 a.m. She asked me if I could pick her up at 9:00 a.m. and run her to the convention center, where she could use their computer and be done before volleyball play began again that afternoon. So early the next morning, I had rustled myself up and out of the sanctuary of my air-conditioned hotel with its crispy sheets, magazines, and hot pot of coffee and faithfully arrived at the dorms across town by 9:00 a.m., only to be told by the chaperone on duty that my daughter was sound asleep and should not be disturbed because she was up half the night doing her writing on a borrowed laptop.

"Could I see it?" I asked.

"No," I was told. "She won't let anyone see it."

As I was leaving for a few more stolen winks of sleep, Lucy herself stumbled down the hall. "Hi, honey," I said. "Do you remember calling me to be here by nine? It would really have been a nice courtesy to me to let me know you didn't need me after all."

"Sorry, Mom—it was late."

"Can I at least read your story?"

"*No*, Mom. This is *my* thing."

And so it was.

I left in a tiny huff of frustration, feeling fully dismissed, disrespected, disgusted, disregarded, disgruntled, and dissed in every other possible way. However, when I read the article the next day, when it appeared in the paper, it shut me up good:

### Great Sportsmanship Found on Countless Teams

By Lucy Krakow

This may seem like an odd comparison, but you may be surprised by the similarities between the Volleyball Festival and the Special Olympics. Not only the great enthusiasm, but also the fantastic sportsmanship. This idea sprouted in my head one day in church when a speaker was talking about an event called the Special Olympics. The speaker told us a heartwarming story about a girl participant who was winning a running race by many strides, but right before she was about to win, she surprised the whole audience by stopping and waiting for the others in the race. She waited until they were right next to her and then they all finished together like a team. Later, when an interviewer questioned her actions, she happily replied, "It is so much more fun to finish with everybody instead of just finishing all alone."

When I heard this, I could not help but smile to myself and think how much that type of great sportsmanship is shown in countless volleyball teams, including my own, at the Volleyball Festival. If you just walk around the different playing centers, you, too, would probably notice it. Whenever anyone shanks a ball or hits into the net, everyone is sure to run to the middle and make sure that person knows it's OK and she can do it while offering an encouraging smile, so quite a bit of weight is lifted off their backs and they can get back to playing their sport to the best of their ability. I know when I mess up and feel down in the dumps, it helps me when the sidelines are still cheering me on saying "good try!" or "you can get that next time!" as if I hardly even played poorly while everybody on the court rushes in to slap high fives with me.

It also helps a person's ability to play when they do not have to deal with a load of self-doubt on their shoulders. It would be so hard to have to play thinking that your team is disappointed in you. These ideas strike other memories in my mind of stories I have heard about the Special Olympics. For example, a group of participants would be successfully running a race, and somebody would trip or fall. Everybody would stop what they were doing to help that person up. They would encourage the person and make sure they know they are doing great. This is the type of attitude that will get a person far in life. It is so much more important to care about the team instead of only thinking that you can win the game alone. That is one of the many reasons so many girls love the sport. Not only is the activity itself incredibly uplifting, but our teams are all there to make it better when we need it most.

Although not many people would think about Special Olympics while playing volleyball, you would be surprised how much it reminds you that your team needs you and you need them to be able to succeed on and off the court.

Wow.

So often I wonder what the heck God was thinking when he paired up teenagers with their amped-up surging hormones and sharp fresh brains with fuzzy-thinking middle-aged moms in the throes of menopause, which for me had been like PMS-ing for years. If I really slow down to ponder it, it becomes so clear teenagers treat their parents pretty much exactly like most humans treat God. In a moment of crisis, when they really need something, they might just give you the time of day, but most of the time, the gifts and the sacrifices get completely obliterated by the incredibly self-absorbed agenda of the humanoid. I get it! Help me! Change me! Hold me tight and never let me go!

Wow.

I love Anna Quindlen for this essay:

## Goodbye Dr. Spock

All my babies are gone now. I say this not in sorrow but in disbelief. I take great satisfaction in what I have today: three almost-adults, two taller than I am, one closing in fast. Three people who read the same books I do and have learned not to be afraid of disagreeing with me in their opinion of them, who sometimes tell vulgar jokes that make me laugh until I choke and cry, who need razor blades and shower gel and privacy, who want to keep their doors closed more than I like. Who, miraculously, go to the bathroom, zip up their jackets and move food from plate to mouth all by themselves. Like the trick soap I bought for the bathroom with a rubber ducky at its center, the baby is buried deep within each, barely discernible except through the unreliable haze of the past. Everything in all the books I once pored over is finished for me now. Penelope Leach, T. Berry Brazelton, Dr. Spock. The ones on sibling rivalry and sleeping through the night and early-childhood education have all grown obsolete. Along with Goodnight Moon and Where the Wild Things Are, they are battered, spotted, well used. But I suspect that if you flipped the pages dust would rise like memories. What those books taught me, finally, and what the women on the playground taught me, and the well-meaning relations—what they taught me, was that they couldn't really teach me very much at all. Raising children is presented at first as a true-false test, then becomes multiple choice, until finally, far along, you realize that it is an endless essay. No one knows anything. One child responds well to positive reinforcement, another can be managed only with a stern voice and a timeout. One child is toilet trained at 3, his sibling at 2. When my first child was born, parents were told to put baby to bed on his belly so that he would not choke on his own spit-up. By the time my last arrived, babies were put down on their backs because of research on sudden infant death syndrome. To a new parent this ever-shifting certainty is terrifying, and then soothing. Eventually you must learn to trust yourself. Eventually the research will follow. I remember 15 years ago poring over one of Dr. Brazelton's wonderful books on child development, in which he describes three different sorts of infants: average, quiet, and active. I was looking for a sub-quiet codicil for an 18-month-old who did not walk. Was there something wrong with his fat little legs? Was there something wrong with his tiny little mind? Was he developmentally delayed, physically challenged? Was I insane? Last year he went to China. Next year he goes to college. He can talk just fine. He can walk, too. Every part of raising children is humbling, too. Believe me, mistakes were made. They have all been enshrined in the "Remember-When-Mom-Did Hall of Fame." The outbursts, the temper tantrums, the bad language, mine, not theirs. The times the baby fell off the bed. The times I arrived late for preschool pickup. The nightmare sleepover. The horrible summer camp. The day when the youngest came barreling out of the classroom with a 98 on her geography test, and I responded, "What did you get wrong?" (She insisted I include that.) The time I ordered food at the McDonald's drive-through speaker and then drove away without picking it up from the window. (They all insisted I include that.) I did not allow them to watch the Simpsons for the first two seasons. What was I thinking? But the biggest mistake I made is the one that most of us make while doing this. I did not live in the moment enough. This is particularly clear now that the moment is gone, captured only in photographs. There is one picture of the three of them, sitting in the grass on a quilt in the shadow of the swing set on a summer day, ages 6, 4 and 1. And I wish I could remember what we ate, and what we talked about, and how they sounded, and how they looked when they slept that night. I wish I had not been in such a hurry to get on to the next thing: dinner, bath, book, bed. I wish I had treasured the doing a little more and the getting it done a little less. Even today I'm not sure what worked and what didn't, what was me and what was simply life. When they were very small, I suppose I thought someday they would become who they were because of what I'd done. Now I suspect they simply grew into their true selves because they demanded in a thousand ways that I back off and let them be. The books said to be relaxed and I was often tense, matter-of-fact and I was sometimes over the top. And

> look how it all turned out. I wound up with the three people I like best in the world, who have done more than anyone to excavate my essential humanity. That's what the books never told me. I was bound and determined to learn from the experts. It just took me a while to figure out who the experts were.*

Wow.

So we basically had just one year left of the four of us living under the same roof together. I decided to stop striving so hard to get it right, threw my agenda out the window, and simply looked for common ground wherever I could find it. I set a goal to pray more, read the Bible more, lighten up, and laugh. On my refrigerator was this slogan: "Contentment is an attitude that we learn, not something we achieve. Be teachable." I put it there for my kids, but of course I so need it for myself, and with any luck I might have a shot at modeling what I want to see in them myself. What a concept.

I tried to listen more and talk less—with my kids and with God—because they, along with my dog Sky, were the best teachers. Doing my job right meant being creative every day and being willing to throw out all the skills that were working for me a few weeks ago and bringing out a fresh new set of skills and creative energy the next week. It meant having the ability to wear one mommy-hat with the strong-willed, quirky, free-spirited, rugged individual girl, and a completely different disguise with the low-key, creative, musical athletic dude with the rich imaginary life who described himself as kinda lazy . . . all that without losing my marbles . . . and if you'll remember, we have already established I have no marbles to begin with.

* Anna Quindlen, *Loud and Clear*, 1st ed. Random House, 2004, p. 7. Reprinted by permission from the author.

# Growing Pains

*A preachy, long-winded letter, following a particularly bad and yet typical teenager moment:*

Dear Rog,

It's been a long time since I have written you one of these letters. One of the things I know for sure about myself is that I am verbal-communicationally challenged, but somehow by writing things down I can organize my thoughts better. My thoughts tend to haunt me at three in the morning if they go unexpressed, and I have got to let them out on paper so I can sleep again. The thing I most want you to know is that I am always in your corner, loving you unconditionally, and wanting the best for you. I want you not to feel my judgment or condemnation but that *truly* Dad and I are on your team, wanting to be your first call for help, and someone you can talk to and be honest with. As awful as Friday night was for all of us, I want us all to feel we learned something valuable from it, and that can only be positive. I need to know for sure that if you are ever in a bad situation again, you will not hesitate to call Dad or me again, and we will drop anything to rescue you, and be grateful for that opportunity.

There are so many pressures in the world today . . . the world's values are not usually God's values . . . Do you realize how *lucky* we are that we can hear God's voice in this crazy world? Not so very many people can . . . it is an awesome thing. It is the source of all good things. The thing about getting to do life with God is that he is *everywhere,* and *he* has *all* the answers. The Bible says, "He who has begun a good work in you will complete it." I love that one because it says to me, we are on this adventure called life together; you can try to run, but I will find you because I am God, and you are *not.* He's got your back. When you guys were getting out of control Friday night, God literally screamed in my head so I wouldn't miss it, "GO GET ROGER NOW!" It kind of takes my breath away . . . I am so grateful when I can hear God's voice and literally feel his touch like I did in that fun dream I had about God this week when he woke me up by playfully wiggling my toe after that magical dream I told you about where God took me on an adventure, mattress and all, like Aladdin's carpet flying me through a quick overview of all the adventures and fun he had in store for my life. It was so 3-D, and it reminded me of the experience you had when you watched the movie *The Passion of the Christ.* When the cross was turned over and the blood was dripping from Jesus on that big screen, you told Dad that you felt a drop of his blood on your arm, and it was warm and thick and so real that it kind of freaked you out . . . wowza. Hold on to that defining moment—it was a love letter from God. Don't ever doubt that he is with you and for you. He has all the answers and wisdom you will ever need.

Speaking of wisdom, I wanted to ask you the question, what do *you* think we should do as a consequence for that Friday night rebellion? We all agree that something has got to change from this experience. Getting a haircut is not really a punishment, but let it remind you daily when you look in the mirror you see a different person . . . more grown up . . . wiser from another of life's battles . . . symbolic of a new day, a fresh start. Our God is a God of second chances.

Taking your cell phone away is symbolic because it is a privilege that you will miss and want to earn back. It will probably shut down your social life, which is good because you need more time to think about the social pressures you are facing, turn down the noise a bit, and work out a better way to do it. We can only hear God's sweet, quiet voice when we slow down and actively listen for it.

I hope that you will look for work to constructively fill up Friday and

Saturday nights for the time you are grounded. A strong work ethic is placed inside all who follow God, and it needs to be fed . . . because it builds up our confidence and self-respect. Barb and Tracey would love to have you babysit but always think you are too busy, so they stopped asking.

We all need good boundaries in our lives. The world will tell you that religion is a system of rules that limit your freedom, but those of us who dare to invite God into the center of our lives know that faith is the path to true freedom and adventure—like a kite that can only fly if it is attached to something bigger and stronger. People who do drugs and abuse alcohol think they are being free but are actually actively marching themselves into a hellish prison . . . killing their brain cells by the millions, limiting their future, dimming their dreams and creativity, depressing their ambition, playing Russian roulette with their lives.

My prayer for you is that you will develop the ability to make smart choices and that you will have the daring to invite God to use you to make a difference in this world: to stand up for a better way to do life, to give you the courage and wisdom to take the road less traveled, to recognize truth, and to follow the light and not the darkness. Spend time with people and activities that lift you up, not drag you down. Hold on to your sense of humor and enjoy the journey . . . keep that "Rog-senior-ness" alive in you, declaring every day a beautiful day . . . it has a way of following that direction if you do.

You have been so blessed with natural abilities, but now is the time in your life to really invest in those things and not just passively expect them to be delivered up to you like breakfast in bed. You are athletically gifted, but you rarely work on those skills independently to achieve the next level of excellence. Set some constructive goals for this time so you can feel change happening, for example: I will run one morning each weekend, I will practice my shooting skills twice a week, I will call someone to play tennis once or twice a week so I can impress Buck on Thursdays. (Have good role models that you can emulate, like Buck, your two wonderful grandpas, and of course Jesus! And take *active* steps to let their examples inspire your life.) You are so musically gifted . . . it just thrills me to death to see you writing music and playing in your bands.

And I can't tell you how blown away Dad and I were when you declared your intention to make straight A's. Reassess how you are doing on that goal before it's the last minute: Are there any teachers you need to meet with? Any extra credit you could do to bring those C's up? Could you use a tutor to help you write your next paper? (I just heard about a fantastic guy who just graduated from Harvard and is tutoring kids affordably if you are open to some coaching.) Did you know it is actually a sign of strength and wisdom to ask for help? I only really learned that recently, I am ashamed to say. But don't be burdened by such an ambitious goal of straight A's . . . just know that it's a healthy practice to have high standards for yourself, and unless we set high goals, they don't have a prayer of coming true.

Let's use this time as a wake-up call to do things differently from this day forward. They say the very definition of insanity is doing the same thing over and over again but expecting a different outcome. My greatest hope is that you will not be a pack follower but be a bold, true original . . . that you will like yourself and believe in yourself enough to follow your own path, a path created especially for you by a God who knows you and loves you perfectly, and who needs you to be uniquely *you* for a reason, for an inspired purpose. Be a person of truth and character and high moral standards, and you will have a wonderful life.

It is so easy to get overstimulated in this world with too much coming at you. (I really hope this long letter is not one of those things!) I am so impressed with the leadership role you have taken with the Wednesday-night high school boys' group. It thrills me to see you reading your Bible regularly . . . I confess that sometimes the Bible is so huge that it overwhelms me, but then I remember the essence of the Bible is to love God with all your heart, and to love others as yourself . . . and then the rest falls into place. I really love having your friends over, and I hope you feel free to invite them over here for sleepovers on the trampoline, play Ping-Pong, and go out for pizza and movies or whatever.

Dad and I are anxious always for your feedback on any of this. Being the best parents we can be is the most important job we will ever have, and we don't want to blow it. Fortunately, God is ultimately the perfect parent . . . and if we can all stay fully connected to him, he promises, "I will work all things for the good for those who love me."

We love you very much.

Mom and Dad

# Living Dangerously

For as long as I can remember, I have felt as if live in a strange, not unpleasant, parallel universe apart from much of the world, and in my exploration of spirituality, I have come to find great blessing and meaning and understanding in that . . . "This world is not your true home," God assures me, whispering in confidence that he allowed that in me on purpose—to set me apart for himself . . . so I would so obviously have to admit my need for him and all his wisdom and miracles and magic . . . to keep me from boring myself to tears in the merry-go-round of suburban life.

I have always loved stories, and I know for sure that God loves a good story because he writes one up for each of us billions of people on the earth every day, and his bestselling book is full of over-the-top stories of ordinary people doing extraordinary things. I daydreamed a lot about becoming a writer when I was younger, but when the time came to try to make a living, I had to be honest: Absolutely nothing had ever happened to me. I'd had a sheltered existence in a small beach town where people mostly loved each other and fun just sort of organically happened all around. So right out of college, I opted to work in fundraising, to raise money to try to solve all the world's problems, which sounded easier than writing about nothingness. But it was one of those "Be careful what you wish for" things.

Soon the tornado began to whirl around me, and I have been trying to get a handle on it ever since. Finding the time and quiet space to chronicle life's perfect moments has been a crapshoot at best.

When my mom died so suddenly, I began to finally get rebellious. The Goody Two-shoes complex I'd lived under so much of my life clearly had to go. I still cannot believe some of the things I did and lived to talk about. Sure, they are funny and make a good story, but I believe there is a decent chance I could still be arrested for many of them, and I felt a desperate need to stay out of jail at least until I got my teenagers through the minefield of adolescence.

I was forty-three when I began to write about my freakish year of seven funerals. I was twenty-three in that earlier monsoon season when I began my first year of living dangerously all on my own. I broke my back skiing, men were breaking my heart every chance they got, and then Mom died, and life as I knew it was upended. I was the age my mom was when she got married. It was also the year Caryn, one of my best friends from my high school, got married, and then my other best friend, Amy, got married that same summer. And then that boy next door that I had loved since I first felt my adolescent hormones stirring kissed me one last time and went off to get married. It was hard for me to rejoice at these weddings, because they occurred in such quick succession my head was spinning and because it drove home my own secret fear that I would never ever be able to figure out the game for myself. And then my precious girlfriend that I grew up with across the street—the kind of loyal friend who had talked me down out of a thousand trees, trying to figure out life and boys and great books and our parents dying the same year—wrote me a very delicately worded letter telling me that she was gay. I called her back immediately and blurted out that for heaven's sake, she was as gay as I was!

Did those words just escape my lips? Is that why I always had so many terrific girlfriends and could never quite figure out the boyfriend deal? Needless to say, it was a fresh new subject for pondering at 3:00 in the morning. Could something possibly be trying to tell me in all this that *I was gay*?

Note to self: *Shut up and listen 'cause this is important, and I am only going to say it once*: Sometimes things happen in your life, and you are supposed to just listen and receive it and not try to make it all about *you*.

I guess I was just so confused by how much I loved her and thought I knew about her. I had watched her try to flirt for years, but the guys who asked her out were always so beneath her. She was athletic and smart and so wise and highly evolved. And now she had someone to love and was setting up house with another great woman. They went on to create a beautiful family together, complete with two heroic adoption rescues: a spunky little girl from China and a sweet boy from Cambodia. It seemed to make so much sense . . . we are not wired up to make it in life as a solo act. I think she is extraordinary, and I fervently pray that the fundamentalist church folks will get over their misguided perception of gay marriage as somehow a threat. The God that I know is more than capable of meeting each person right where they are, just as he created them. This politicized hot potato is such an evil diversion, ideally suited to set the church up to shoot itself in the foot, divide people, and distract us from what matters in this life. To quote the theme from the movie *The Year of Living Dangerously* and also my life: "Why can't we simply learn to love?"

At that stage in my life, I was so sick and tired of my own company and even sicker and tireder of the way men behaved toward me. The lovely Italian (*married! Hello!*) professor was still romancing me from afar, with letters and poetry and phone calls, and I was still reeling from a romantic snafu with that ski lobbyist who pretended to love me for a spell. My heart was just imploding all the time, and my spirit kind of broke under the strain of all the changes, and so I opted to drop out for a while.

The years following mom's loss were a lonely, lonely time. And sad, sad, sad. In our family we all mourned separately because we instinctively knew we would only compound each other's pain and loss if we shared it. Mom left each of us a little money in a life insurance policy, so I could drift a bit. I was successfully earning almost a living and enjoying the freedom and flexibility of being my own boss (read: unemployable, slightly mental), creating fabulous earrings out of beer bottle caps, marketed as "Beers for the Ears" in San Francisco, and "Go Beers" near the UC Berkeley campus. Each creation was authenticated with a stamp on its packaging "Hand-drunk by the manufacturer" for added prestige.

My old college roommate Gidge was living in LA and had this sexy and exciting job doing TV and fashion shoots for Saks Fifth Avenue. All throughout college she had this boyfriend who was so phony and cocky and arrogant that I could not be trusted to be even remotely civil with him. He was a raging alcoholic, and she got into this cycle of rescuing him in a million ways. Gidge had transferred into Berkeley from a small conservative Midwestern college in the middle of our sophomore year. She dressed crisply every morning in full preppy garb with a starched ribbon in her hair, the likes of which was rarely seen at Berkeley. We became fast friends when she asked me, the morning after a raging party next door, "Exactly how far do boys here expect you to go on a first date here in California?" Apparently, she had been mauled and groped by a drunk guy the night before . . . and I just loved her for asking me that question . . . so flattered was I to think somebody thought I might have an answer. She was a breath of fresh air to me, someone I could be safely naive with, I guess. Unfortunately, that drunk guy became her boyfriend for the next five years, and just trashed her beautiful heart. Their inevitable breakup happened to coincide with my own total eclipse of the heart when Mom died, and so we got to spend time together again picking up the pieces of our shattered hearts and figuring out what ought to happen next.

I'll never forget or forgive Gidge for getting me a gig at the Pasadena Junior League's Fashion Show as a robot/break dancer leading a team of children down the runway. It was truly the most humiliating $100 I ever earned, since I was not then, nor have I ever remotely been, a break dancer. She also got me an appearance on the *A.M. Los Angeles* morning TV show as a "Glamour Don't." Good times, proud moments. I was soon able to convince her that we needed to achieve a complete identity change and go hide our special selves in Europe for a spell—so off we impulsively went, flitting and flirting through England, France, and Italy while our money lasted. On our first day in London, we waltzed right into Wimbledon for free by dropping the name of a friend of ours from Berkeley who was playing doubles there. Another memorable night in Venice, we stayed out too late for our hostel's curfew and had to hunker down all night long under a tarp in a gondola. I will always have a soft spot in my heart for the Gidge who had to put up with me bursting into tears spontaneously throughout that trip whenever something beautiful happened that I could not share with my mom upon my return. And there was so much spectacular beauty there.

The experience of world travel blew my mind and whetted my appetite for more, more, *more*! Unfortunately, I had blown all my money and was in desperate need of rent and food money upon my return. Still somewhat haunted by the foggy, wallowing, hangover of grief, I couldn't fathom what I could do next. My sister had gotten a job as a flight attendant, which meant she could travel the world for free, which sounded so good to me. I tried and tried and tried to get hired by an airline, but somehow, they could see through me—that I was a bit of a wild card who might one day snap, "Why don't you just get over yerself and get yer own dang coffee!"

In the meantime, and I considered it especially mean, my baby brother had graduated from college and oh-so-easily landed a flight-attending job, based in Hawaii, to have some fun before heading off to law school (at least my sister had the decency to be based in Detroit). So when I learned that my two siblings were headed to Cozumel for a sojourn, it seemed like a perfectly super idea to use my sister's extra ID card there on her dresser for a free standby flight to join them. Incredibly, because I am a dead ringer for my sister, I waltzed right onto a flight and enjoyed a fun-filled free vacation. Remember the days of innocence and no security tactics before 9/11? Alas, in my life, God is so faithful to let no bad deed go unnoticed, so on my return flight homeward, I was coincidentally seated next to the campaign manager for Pat Robertson, who was then running for president. He evangelized me relentlessly for five straight hours. He absolutely hammered me on my liberal view of homosexuality and the AIDS crisis and showed me everything I needed to know about how not to be an effective evangelist in one crash course . . . and believe me, at times I was fervently praying for the plane to crash, during the longest five hours of my life. It was so God's brilliant sense of humor. You would have thought that little experience would have taught me a valuable lesson about abiding by the law, but I was just so *fed up* with being a good girl. It seemed like such a lie, and a bore, and so much *work*, and I felt so frustrated and rejected by the airline industry, such an unemployable loser, that I continued with my crime spree a year later when another juicy opportunity presented itself.

I had met my one true love by this time. We were planning to meet up with my sister and her best flying buddy, Elmer (name changed to protect the guilty), at the El Torito restaurant by the airport to toast his last flight before leaving his job for flight school to become a pilot. Unfortunately, my one true love had made previous plans to stop by a client's party after work, where he confessed it was likely he would run into his old girlfriend of the past three years. That might have threatened me, if I wasn't so supremely confident that I was such a catch myself. We planned to meet up in a couple of hours in Margaritaville.

Hours went by, and when my one true love finally showed up to join us at the restaurant, I was in a bit of a puddle, having imagined him off sharing a bottle of champagne with his old girlfriend and falling madly back in love. He reassured me immediately he was simply late due to traffic, and we all had a fun, very memorable dinner and quite a few large margaritas together. In fact, we were all surprised to note that the time was 11:00 p.m., and we had barely enough time to scoot back to the airport for the red-eye back to Detroit.

"Hey! Why don't we *all* go back to Detroit together?" one of us geniuses suggested.

After all, the flight was practically empty, and my sister's job was to take tickets, and since we had never even been to Motown, it seemed like a superb plan! We quickly devised a plan to hand over a couple of blank ticket envelopes that we were to give her as we boarded, as if we were legitimate travelers, and what could be easier? No harm, no foul, right? Anyone not under the hallucinogenic influence of tequila could see that this was a plan doomed for failure. Alas, we are the kind of people who tend to learn our lessons the hard way.

We decided we would board the plane separately, to avoid any suspicion. I repaired to the ladies' room, as my one true love went on ahead. I was shocked by my reflection in the bathroom mirror and took great pains to redo my face to look like someone who had actually been planning to go to Detroit and not something that had been dragged in sideways by the cat. As previously stated, my concept of time had been seriously tweaked by copious amounts of tequila, so as I flounced out of the ladies' room, all foofed up and ready to go, I encountered a strange (*so* not *my friendly sister!),* severe-looking gate agent closing down the Jetway.

"Wait!" I shouted. "My sister is on that flight, and I have got to get a message to her!" But the gate agent was on a schedule and so not impressed with me. Alas, off the three of them went into the night sky to Detroit . . . without me. And because Roger had the car keys in his pocket (and I had no business driving anyway), it was a very long bus ride home alone. I swore off my life of crime forever.

On board the aircraft, my sister began to perform her informative drills for her five sleepy passengers and her one tipsy stowaway. Roger innocently assumed I had been seated in first class as the plane pulled away and was horrified to learn from my pale, very tense sister that I had not quite made the flight. My sister later told me he was inconsolable, blathering that he had never missed me or loved me so much in his whole sorry life. (How can I miss you if you never go away?) So she plied him with a stiff drink up there in the deserted first-class section, and to cheer him up, she let him live out his own flight-attending fantasy, wearing her jacket and scarf and serving drinks to the five unreceptive slumbering passengers. Just when they were about to arrive in Detroit, he began to realize that the nasty cocktails he'd had after work, combined with the margaritas we'd had together and the bracing B-52 mystery drink they'd mixed him to help him cope with the sickening realization that he was going to Detroit by accident, had all conspired in his stomach to do a little vigilante justice of their own. Roger raced to the latrine, where his six-foot-six frame attempted to drive the proverbial porcelain bus. Unfortunately, even in relative luxury of first class, it is impossible for someone of that stature to hurl successfully, so he opted to sit on the commode and tried to throw up into the sink, which had the nastiest way of swirling and flipping the chunks right back onto his jean jacket. When the plane landed and my sister began to search frantically for him, he was ultimately easily located by the foul odor emanating from the first-class bathroom. She was now very afraid she was going to be discovered and fired and/or sent to jail, so she distanced herself from the stowaway, hissing under her breath, "I'll meet you in baggage claim in fifteen minutes! Get outta here!"

It sounded simple enough, but it was a large, strange airport, and he had perhaps killed off so many brain cells that night that he could not properly read the signage and instead stumbled along the endless corridors and ended up in the international flights' baggage claim area, where he perched himself lamely like so much unclaimed luggage for what felt like hours. He later recalled a particularly humiliating incident where a mother with young innocent children navigated a noticeably wide berth around him, as if he obviously carried the threat of some vile or contagious disease. Miraculously my sister eventually found him and got him home, where he could bundle up in her fluffy robe and phone me at last, waking me up to a shrieking, semihysterical cry, "I'm in *Detroit*!"

It was a hangover to remember, and we have all straightened up and flown right ever since. Very pricey one-way return ticket from Mr. Toad's-Wild-Ride-free-trip-to-Detroit. Lesson learned. Mission accomplished. No need to prosecute . . . surely the statute of limitations has *got* to have expired by now, and the aviation world is now a warmer, cozier, safer place to be for all . . . oh yeah.

# City of Doomed Lovers

Once upon a time, there was a tortured English major who would like to remain anonymous for the purposes of this tale. She had been dating her true love for two years, and it had become increasingly obvious that he was never, *ever* going to propose marriage, since as next-door neighbors they were essentially cohabitating happily enough ever after, so what was the big deal? As if taking her cue from the misguided machinations of fair Juliet and her Romeo, our heroine conceived a mature plot to run dramatically away from home to Italy to shake things up and see if her lover noticed any significant loss.

My spinster sister and I dared Dad to join us on short notice, on an Italian adventure, to steep our parched selves in the magic of the Italian culture of romance and wine and food and all good things, for as long as we could stretch our meager budgets. We found an amazing apartment full of antiques for twelve dollars a night, hanging out over the cliffs of the Cinque Terre—five car-free villages joined by the Via del Amore ("the walk of love"), a winding five-mile path carved precariously into the rocky coastline, bounded on either side by vineyards and the Mediterranean Sea. It has *got* to be the most romantic place on earth . . . and there I was with my dad and sister. It is truly amazing how my manipulative plans faithfully double back on me and slap me on the fanny. My one true love, never one to cling, had sent me off on my big adventure with his blessing, asking me to call him in a couple of weeks to see if he might be able to get away from work and meet up with us for a Mediterranean moment.

Refreshed and inspired by our adventures, I did call him one morning to check in. It was early, and I woke him from a dead sleep. He happily announced he had indeed purchased a ticket to Italy and would be arriving in a few days. I gave him directions to our apartment as best I could, telling him when he arrived in Milan, he should take a train for the coast and then transfer in Genoa to one of the local southbound trains to the village of Rio Maggiore, which is just a speck on most maps, located just south of Genoa and north of La Spezia. He should plan to head into the village and ask for Lorenzo at the café in the little marina, which also rented apartments. My one true love is never too sharp in the morning, and in hindsight I can imagine him scrawling these notes without the aid of his contact lenses. I should have known something would get lost in translation.

He was to arrive in Milan at 9:00 a.m. I calculated an hour to the coast plus an hour buffer and no more than twenty minutes on the local train, which ran through town every hour on the half. I began meeting each train starting at 11:30 a.m.—no small feat as that foolhardy act of love slavery entailed scaling punishing granite steps up and over a mountain and back each time. Ultimately, I made seven trips, wilting more and more by the hour . . . and there was never anyone that I could engage in a passionate embrace on board. Dad and Sis and I were drinking perhaps too much of the sweet, fresh fruity wine of the region to try to numb my sheer desperation. As the seventh half hour approached, I dared myself to make one last stand . . . and when to my utter disbelief, my one true love emerged from that train, armed with a bouquet of wilty flowers, I greeted him lovingly with a shriek: *"Where on earth have you been?"*

"I'm thrilled to see you, too, Sweetie," he said gamely as he gathered my overwrought, exhausted self into his mercifully understanding, unconditionally loving arms. My heart exploded with joy, just flooded with love and laughter, as he told the story of delay after delay and trying to communicate with the Italian nuns on the train, who pantomimed that he was going north when he needed to be going south, and now here he was (the one with the jet lag) carting me back up and down the granite torture stairs one last time. We had a most wonderful dinner in the marina that night, with a giant seafood platter full of fresh calamari tentacles and mussels and things my Americanized dad never thought he would be caught dead eating, let alone enjoying.

In the evenings we would wander along the Via del Amore, watching the firefly show and making out passionately on hot summer nights that were something out of a steamy romance novel . . . not quite real life. Roger later confessed that it was there that he first felt the impulse to pop the *big* question, but he bravely squelched the impulse . . . much to my peril. It could have been such a great story to tell our grandchildren. Instead, we would skulk back to our twin beds in our little apartment shared with my dad and sister.

After several days of this relentlessly obnoxious magic, we boldly decided to move on to explore new sights and make our way up to the Italian Alps to visit my uncle Bob and his sweetheart, Rosetta. We were headed to spend one night in Verona, which for me shall heretofore always be followed by the picture-postcard tagline "City of Doomed Lovers," because I will never, *ever*, get over what went down there.

We had to change trains in Milan. There was half an hour between trains, so we all scattered to change money, get food for a picnic, go to the bathroom, etc., and were to meet back at track number twelve. Three of us met up easily, but Dad went completely AWOL. We fanned out on the train, hoping he had found a seat, but came up empty. As the train began to pull away, we spotted him in the station, looking confused.

*"Run!"* we screamed. But he didn't budge.

Poor Dad. It later turned out that we had his passport and his train ticket, so he couldn't change money, and it all completely overwhelmed his brain. It ended up taking several minor miracles for him to catch a train. We didn't know this then, so all we could think of to do was to meet the next two trains from Milan . . . and were absolutely confounded when he didn't disembark. We decided to leave yellow Post-it notes all over the station, directing Dad to the pensione we had found nearby. We checked into two rooms and desperately went out to grab a late dinner and some wine to help us process this ridiculous dilemma.

"I can't *believe* we lost *Dad*!" We pondered every possible scenario. Should we contact the police? Perhaps he would just make his way to Uncle Bob's house, and we would meet up there. He also had his best friends from college staying in Lake Como; could he have run into them?

As we stumbled home, full of angst, my sister insisted that my one true love and I take the upstairs room. We had been so desperate to be alone together, and under such dire circumstances were in need of creative comfort.

Miraculously, through the kindness of strangers, Dad arrived in the middle of the night, and the front desk placed him in the room with my sleeping sister, who awoke the next morning with a splitting headache and asked my dad to go upstairs and ask me for an aspirin. She had obviously killed all her brain cells the night before and was not to be trusted. Dad opened the door at the top of the stairs thinking it was a hallway, but in fact it was the door to our room, which we had thought was locked, leading him right smack into a scene that no father should ever have to see . . . right there in broad daylight . . . on top of the covers . . . how do you say, "in flagrante delicto?" (*translation*: nothing whatsoever left to the imagination).

Dad froze. Dumbstruck. My one true love actually had to yell the words "*Close the door*!" as my poor shell-shocked dad mumbled, "I thought this was the hallway . . ." in apology.

As I write this, it has been nearly several decades since the scene played out, and words to describe my reaction to it still cannot do the moment justice. Think: Edward Munch's painting *The Silent Scream* . . . now there's a picture worth a thousand words. After Dad shut the door, my twisted mind raced paradoxically to my favorite movie from childhood, *The Sound of Music* . . . I could race over and catch the first train to Salzburg, find a convent, get an identity change, and become a nun, like Fräulein Maria. I needed that kind of redemption . . . plus, I never wanted to see anyone I knew and loved ever again. This little love affair of mine? I was so *over* it. So done. That much was painfully clear. I just imploded with embarrassment and regret and humiliation. On the best of days, I seemed to have no tangible coping skills and *way* too many nerve endings too close to the surface to be a functioning grown-up human being.

I feel every insult like a dagger to the heart, and *this* . . . well, this felt like the final, ultimate insult. I thought of the tragedy of Romeo and Juliet, and this accursed town . . . and I felt such a perverse kinship.

Out of the wretched gloom, a voice was saying, "I'm going to go downstairs and try to talk to your dad." A naked body was stepping into pants.

"Right," I said sarcastically. "What can you possibly say?"

"I don't know. But it's got to be done."

"Well—you tell him we had planned to be married someday!" I blathered . . . as if that would make a difference.

He thoughtfully zipped up his fly, put on a shirt, and left me in my silent-scream mode for over forty-five minutes . . . plenty of time to spontaneously combust. My imagination is a dangerous place to be on a good day, but under these conditions, I shudder to elaborate further.

Suffice to say, I was immobilized by a cornucopia of images to fuel my misery. A giddy array of my life's countless most-embarrassing moments compounded and galloped gleefully before my eyes, like a mocking polar opposite of the movie *It's a Wonderful Life*: the time my twelve-year-old self got up in the middle of the night to go to the bathroom while sleeping overnight at the home of my best friend, who had recently lost her mother to cancer, only to stumble sleepily back into bed with her extremely intense, humorless father . . . the time I dared to go to my first raging high school party at sixteen, and I ducked into the bathroom (yet again failing to lock the door!) and in walked the boy who had captured all my adolescent imagination for the prior two years, catching me perched ever-so-daintily with my pants around my ankles on the latrine, and causing me to dread the thought of ever making eye contact with him again . . . the one and only time a boy that I really admired asked me out in college, and I had him on such a pedestal that I felt compelled to drink a couple of cocktails before he picked me up to steel my nerves (in the days before I could discern my limits) and spent the entire evening just sick to my stomach and such a pathetic excuse for a date. Incredibly, the embarrassment factors so elemental in my life so far seemed to compound and build toward this last remaining Paramount Picture's finest climactic (*choice word!*) moment. I was startled to find myself still there when my former one true love entered the room (I definitely was so *over* this love nonsense once and for all). It was all clearly beyond my limited skill set. He said very simply and quietly that he and my dad loved me very much and they had spent most of the past hour discussing how they could help me get through this.

I was stunned. It had never occurred to me before, but in that moment, I realized with absolute certainty that I was perfectly loved. My dad had always been such a rock in my life, such a decent, honest, supportive, true-blue guy. He deserved better than this. I felt so unworthy but was somehow inspired to try to reflect some of that advanced-degree grown-up love back to those guys . . . eventually . . . but first I needed to try to practice breathing normally again. My one true love was back again and in my heart now in a heroic new way. He was my rescuer and my safe place, and he knew of a cute little bar down by the river where we should try to get a bracing drink before rejoining Dad and my traitor-sister on any further travel adventures, the likes of which there are virtually *zero* instructions whatsoever in any travel guidebooks.

Roger and I had never tried grappa before, but we drank it like water that morning, as if hoping to kill off all the brain cells that might cause us to recall the events of this regrettable day. Its searing qualities helped us to burn some distance between us and the ickiness of the past few hours. We vaguely knew that we were going to survive this, and you know how they say those things that do not kill us may actually make us stronger? Hope is a beautiful thing.

When we met up with Dad and my sister later that day, there were hugs and a few awkward words, and a hint that this was going to be something we laughed a lot about later . . . just not yet. We had a nice meal together on an outside patio, and Dad decided to take off for a few days and meet up with his college pals in Lake Como for a break from the unbearable strain of playing father to a twenty-six-year-old infant. We would then rendezvous in Merano, in the Italian Alps, where my uncle Bob and aunt-to-be Rosetta ran a hotel. We fled Verona on the next available train, never, *ever* to return.

We sort of needed to be nowhere for a spell, so we headed aimlessly in the direction of the mountain. We stumbled upon a village at the base of a huge mountain outside Bolzano and learned that we could take a lift all the way up the mountain and stay in a lodge there if we liked. The open-air lift went on for a good half hour or so. It was June and we were dressed in shorts and T-shirts for a summer day, but halfway up the mountain, it began to snow . . . it was so unexpected and refreshing. We arrived at the lodge frozen like Popsicles, but it was a magical wonderland oasis, where we were warmly greeted with hot spiced wine, fondue, and fluffy down beds. We were their only guests, and we thought we had died and gone to heaven.

The next day we headed to Merano and the comforts of family who loved us and knew absolutely nothing about Verona. We were warmly greeted by Rosetta and her sister, who had run the Hotel Merano as a family business for most of their lives. Rosie speaks Italian and German and only a "leetle" broken English with her chirpy musical Italian accent. We introduced ourselves for the first time, and she appeared overwhelmed with emotion as she addressed Roger and me.

"And you, are zee lovers?"

I blushed, imagining that the news had somehow beat us from Verona to make the front page of the *Merano News Press*.

"You will, you must . . . the best room by the river," chirped Rosetta.

The room we shared there was an absolute sanctuary; the roar of the rushing river outside was deafening, soothing . . . at last, peace like a river (the poetic title of one of my all-time favorite books by Leif Enger). We were pampered and rested and restored by the time Dad arrived a few days later, and Rosie discreetly put him into his very own room, far away from ours so he didn't have to deal with the insidious "Verona factor." And in many ways, we all put the whole unfortunate incident to bed, so to speak. In general Italy is such an incredible place for lovers; I just strongly feel there needs to be better security or some sort of a traveler's advisory or disclaimer for lovers headed to Verona. So there you have it.

My uncle Bob was quite an extraordinary man. When he was a young man growing up in Czechoslovakia, the Nazis killed his entire family, and he escaped by going to the United States for college. He was of course terribly lonely and heartbroken and one day put an ad in *The New Yorker* personals, which my aunt Doris, my dad's sister, answered. They held an intense correspondence between New York and Los Angeles for many months, which ultimately led to meeting and marriage. My uncle adored her, and shortly after they were married, she learned she had this rare, deadly cancer and that her beautiful, artistic life would not be long. She was told that she should not have children, but her rebellious spirit insisted, and she soon gave birth to my cousin Claire, and together they stared down that cancer with the strength of their indomitable spirits for another thirty years following her diagnosis. When she finally died, just a year before my mom, who also adored her, my uncle Bob was inconsolable. He tried to rally himself to travel a bit to distract himself from his grief. And when he happened upon Rosetta's hotel, and she heard his story, her heart went out to him like an angel of mercy, and he stayed and stayed and stayed.

We, too, loved her immediately. She was a wonderful cook and storyteller. And she has the most extravagant capacity for expressing love. By day we would hike the trails of this beautiful Shangri-la in the Alps, trying to keep up with Uncle Bob, who was always jauntily dressed in a sport coat and dress shoes but somehow could always leave us in his dust in our tennis shoes. Bob would talk and reminisce constantly . . . he never forgot a face, or a detail, as if he were a curator in the great museum of life. I imagine all the losses he suffered in life made what remained that much more vivid and sacred. There was always a castle with an incredible restaurant waiting for us at the end of our trail. And then we would walk home eager to return to Rosetta's cozy kitchen and an eight-course meal, where we invariably hurt her feelings when we couldn't find room to stuff in one more bite of the final cheese platter.

Over dinner we listened to her precious stories. She told us how in the winter, she would keep her basement windows open so the birds could come in out of the cold. She always left them food, and when spring came, some of the birds never left, and one in particular would hop on top of her hat as she walked to the market and perch there proudly like an ornament. We laughed at the perfection of that image: Rosetta, with her lilting voice, the birdwoman of Merano.

When she and I drove Roger to the train station a few days later, I clung to him, saying goodbye as if my life depended on it . . . I was going to miss him like crazy after all we'd been through. He had been such a steadfast rock for me and my wobbly knees and spineless torso to stand on, not to mention such a hunka, hunka burning love. I have long been a big believer in getting right back up on that horse when you fall off.

Rosie took him aside. "You will, to come back, when you are married, yes, and with zee babies?"

We did get back there too . . . with babies aged six and nine, who immediately bonded with their Italian grandparents. And then Uncle Bob ventured out for Christmas the following year, without Rosie the birdwoman, who was ironically terrified of flying. That was the last time we saw him. He died the following year, and now sweet Rosetta remains devastated. We try to communicate via letters. We found an interesting computer program that translates English to Italian but does bizarre things like translate the name Bob as "a ducking, dodging person," so I worry about what messages we are actually sending. Claire told us they scattered Uncle Bob's ashes in the Merano River adjacent to the hotel, against the law, but very much in keeping with his spirit. I send up prayers all the time to that perfect translator in the sky to protect and comfort Rosetta and Claire and to bless Uncle Bob and hold him close. I am so grateful for these precious family members so far away. We wish you peace like a river, Uncle Ducking, Dodging Person.

# Friends

When Mary died, I honestly thought we would have to move. It was just too sad to walk out the front door every day and revisit the offensive news that she was not ever going to be home again. This was my cowardly way of trying to guard my heart from pain. If I didn't have to see her house every day, maybe I could compartmentalize (note the root word: *mental*?) the fact that she was really gone and be able to move on. But then I thought of her kids and how they were soldiering on, reflecting her positive energy and spirit, reminding me that she lived on in them. They were all so plucky and positive and brave that it inspired me to try to emulate that—because that was what she modeled for us all, contagious enthusiasm for life. In an act of defiance against the forces of gravity then threatening to swamp our canoes, we instead decided to add on to our house, so that we might better weather the teen years. Within months, the beautiful blessings began to flow, so abundantly that I could not write it off as a coincidence. Let me try to recount a few highlights:

Every morning Mary's daughter, Sarah, a delightful morning person, would come over before school, like the breath of fresh air that she is, like pure sunshine, and she rustled Lucy out of bed for me, like the sister who has known her and her ways all her life, the sister I wish she had but God so capably provided anyway in his roundabout way. Then we would all do breakfast and the school commute together. They always laughed and giggled, and I got to watch her grow up, and tried to spoil her any way I could, keeping my connection to Mary well fed and very much in the present.

Beautiful artistic Kappy, who brought me homemade cookies that made me cry when the news broke that Mary was dying, became a trusted friend. I remember the gorgeous handmade quilt that she made to keep Mary warm also brought her such tender comfort and spurred many happy tears. Kappy's gift of hospitality and sense of fun and honesty and faith have made life so new and different and full. We have made several trips to work at an orphanage in Tijuana together and have shared life at a heart level for many years now. For my birthday a few years ago, she also gave me one of her paintings, which will probably stand out on my deathbed as one of the most amazingly thoughtful gifts I have ever received.

And just across the street that year, in moved extraordinary Barb, who is so competent and generous and loyal and true. She became that first-call-for-help kind of friend and neighbor that Mary was. She was a powerful, willing backup mommy to my kids, who so needed to see something different from what I modeled for them. Her quiet faith and sensitivity moved mountains that I got to see with my own eyes every day. She is a networking genius, with such a compassionate heart for others that is truly an inspiration, and she is developing the most thrilling direct hotline connection to God. She was a brilliant advocate for middle school kids in a way that I wish I could have been, with grace and truth, so that they did not become discouraged or made to feel like they could not ever do anything right.

Verita, whose name itself means "truth," is a brilliant counselor, theologian, and intellect, with such a tender heart for God and for people. She lost her mother the same year I lost mine, and she just got that about me and has become another sister friend. She is such a fierce prayer warrior and not incidentally deals with multiple sclerosis, but I often forget that is the root of her walking differently because she embodies how it is to walk with God, and her feet just supernaturally do not quite touch the ground the way most people's do anyway.

Debbie—who coached Lucy in volleyball for years before we became friends—loved and evolved those girls over several years through healthy teamwork and that powerful outlet of good clean fun. I was honored that she confided in me about the things on her heart. How intimate and bonding it was to be asked to intercede in prayer for another person, when in my heart of hearts, I had started to believe the lie, that I did not know what the heck I was doing in the prayer department, having prayed so hard for Mary's miracle that was not to be. Deb is not outwardly very social, and I feel so honored that she reached out to me in friendship and confidences. Having raised three great teenagers a couple of years ahead of me, she has been an invaluable sounding board. Her son Jake is a brilliant saxophone player. He loved to play so much that he tweaked some nerves in his arm that was giving him chronic, debilitating pain. The doctors couldn't figure it out, so they cavalierly suggested he pick up a different hobby. Deb researched it better than the doctors, and we prayed and prayed for him, and he persevered and is now a professional touring musician and a walking miracle.

And darling Ann . . . truly the most positive person I had ever met. She made having four teenagers look easy. She looks like a teenager herself, knows how to dress, and is totally hot for her husband after all these years. At first her house appeared to always be clean, and I watched her entertain so effortlessly . . . so I tried *hard* not to like her for all that, but then I took to popping in on her unannounced, demanding coffee or a walk, and I caught her a few times being ever-so-slightly discombobulated, and it humanized her for me. My favorite story about her was the day when we were talking on the phone and she uncharacteristically unleashed on me her frustration that her calendar had gone missing for days and that she was starting to get a little nutty keeping all the balls in the air for her very active family without it. We had been talking about God and life lately on our morning walks, so it felt safe to let her in on my little secret: I am God's czarina of the mundane, and I have an uncanny gift for finding lost things by remembering that while I may not know where the lost thing is, I know someone who always does. The deal is, God does not want to be only your 911 call; he wants to be with you, and for you all day long, in all the details! All you have to do is ask.

I dared her, "Have you prayed about it?" She sent up a quick prayer, and do you know, right as we were talking, she opened up the cabinet door she had looked in a thousand times, and there was the offending calendar! This incident bonded us like nothing else could. Ann started coming to church and our Thursday Bible study group regularly after that one. She was also needing a place to process a fear that had been dogging her: that her darling dad's years were numbered, and she didn't think she could handle that loss; they were so close, so connected. There were numerous near-death experiences, buckets of tears and grief contained, and when he finally passed on, at eighty-nine, she stood up and seamlessly, lovingly spoke the eulogy, saluting her father's extraordinary life with the absolute conviction that she needed no notes, and that God would speak through her. She talked about his life in front of hundreds of people, and the maturity of her faith was a wonder to behold. She spoke so eloquently about her father's last words, framing them in the context that he and his mother were always exceptionally close, and that he had said, "Oh, Mom, it's so beautiful here!" and closed his eyes for the last time with a smile.

Ann had been a devoted daughter, taking her dad and his pals to lunch in San Francisco once a week, enjoying their stories, effortlessly flirting her way into their hearts, and mourning each passing until finally only her dad was left. She knew they had made the most of their time together, that they had truly, madly, deeply loved each other, and that he had gone on to a better place where his body was no longer holding him hostage and where they would meet again someday. Ann is the kind of person people watch and think, "I have got to get me some of that kind of energy and enthusiasm." The key is the more she gives it out, the more it multiplies. She can so casually and confidently point to God as the source of all that good stuff. She makes me want to try to be a better person, not such a grumbler. She moved to Switzerland that year, the same summer as my dear friend Tinker moved to Michigan, the same summer that my Sky-dog died, and my firstborn up and went off to University of Oregon, and I was missing them all something fierce.

I am eager for the pain of it all to teach me something very valuable about this human experience. Indeed pain is the common experience of the birth process and the dying process . . . and it seems to influence everything in between to some degree. I like that image of life as the "dash" mark between the obligatory two dates on a headstone in the cemetery . . . unfortunately, too many of us take that "dash" literally and miss so many sacred moments along the way because we fail to build in margins, and the beauty gets dimmed by the adrenaline-junkie warp-speed pace of our lives. Life *is* deadly—100 percent of the time—it's what we do with that life that counts. I absolutely adore Randy Pausch for sharing his contagious passion for life with us all in his book *The Last Lecture*. And I felt the same way after reading *Tuesdays with Morrie*, by Mitch Albom. Please, God, let me have that kind of character at the end of this race.

My friend Paula, who was staring down a deadly disease while raising two teenagers as a single mother, told me the story of how she'd felt God romancing her, ever since she was an eight-year-old kid, in a classic illustration of childlike faith. She was sitting on a mountaintop with her cousin talking about deep stuff, and when she learned that her cousin didn't believe in God, she screeched, "Oh, you have to believe in God! If you do, you can get pretty much anything you want! Watch this, I'll pray: God, please bring us some butterflies." And within moments, a massive swarm of beauties enfolded them and just blew both their minds. It is a memory that has inspired the rest of her life, which was unbelievably rough, featuring an alcoholic absentee mother and an abusive husband who abandoned her and left her destitute with twin babies. That powerful butterfly memory has shored her up many times when she dared to doubt God's absolute favor and protection and provision. Somehow along the way in our butterfly existence, we emerge from childhood's cocoon and lose or unlearn or doubt that kind of pure trusting connection with God and all his majestic mysteries.

And I remain fiercely loyal to my Cal kibbutz mates—Anne, Gidge, Carey, Deb, Carol, Melissa, Kathy and Kathryn—all smart, funny, ambitious women who helped raise my game and navigate the absolute minefield of late adolescence into independence, with so much laughter and so many blackmail-worthy memories from Berkeley and beyond.

Final shout-out to my friend and neighbor Lori, mother of five (count 'em:

*five!*), who loved to run me down with her gigantic car as she flew by my house on her loops. We took up Rollerblading together in an attempt to reclaim our girlish figures, but we never quite figured out how to use our brakes, so our days may be numbered. She never failed to make me laugh. She dubbed me the "patron saint of flailing birdlings" since I made her help me duckling-proof all the storm drains in our neighborhood for a different kind of fun and exercise. It is one of my favorite stories.

When fluky things happen once, it is easy enough to write it off as a wild and crazy day, but when things happen repeatedly, it gets my attention. There I was on mommy-field-trip duty, shepherding thirty fifth graders to hear an author speak at our beloved independent bookstore, Book Passage, a mere six blocks away. It all seemed right up my alley when I volunteered, but we faced unexpected sideways-driving rains on the day of the walking field trip. Picture four classrooms of thirty lightweight kids dressed in Glad trash bags with a hole punched in the bottom for their heads to fit through, walking purposefully to the bookstore. On the long, damp walk home, we startled a mother duck and her brand-new babies wandering back to the lagoon nearby. The kids got them excited, and they scattered, and I watched helplessly as the frantic ducklings stumbled down the storm drains and into hedges. *Chaos*. The teachers herded the kids back to school, but I stayed on, and I spent the better part of an hour coaxing several out of the storm drain and another out of the bushes and on toward the mother duck, who was squawking and in a big hurry to get to the lagoon with at least most of her babies. I was drenched to the bone, but I could still hear a faint peeping in the hedge. One of the other moms and her young daughter came back to try to help. We found a hockey stick and poked the dense shrubbery, trying in vain to flush the duckling out. The peeping was getting fainter and fainter; the poor thing was so exhausted. I knew I couldn't give up and still respect myself in the morning, so I sent up a quick prayer of "*Help!*" It's powerful, easy to remember, so handy for so many things . . . you simply *must* try it sometime!

I soon saw the little yellow fluff ball panting under a branch and pounced as gently yet firmly as I could. Success! We swept the duckling off to the nearby

Wild Care center for rehabilitation, since his mother had long since abandoned us. A photo was snapped of the adorable little girl who helped us, holding the baby duckling, and it appeared on the cover of our local newspaper, poetically just in time for its Easter week publication.

I could hardly contain my euphoria! In that space of an hour down on my hands and knees wrangling ducklings in a rainstorm, I had such an amusing moment of intimacy with God. I was emotional about the waste of losing even one of those adorable chirpers to the gutters of life. I so identified with that mother duck hedging her bets between waiting for all the babies to be safely returned to her and just wanting to give up and make for the lagoon. I told God that I didn't think I could walk away from this seemingly impossible duckling chase and that he was going to have to work this thing out . . . and the minute I surrendered trying to muscle it through in my own pathetic power, he let me capture the wayward duckling. It felt like a huge miracle at the time . . . such a Good Friday story morphing into Easter Sunday liberation.

I was dangerously cold to the bone and couldn't stop shaking, even when the warmth of the bathtub finally surrounded me. A hundred people had seen this miniature disaster, and I was the only one who couldn't walk away. I had been praying that God might find a way to use me in some small way while I was on this alien planet, and this seemed like the first sign of an answered prayer. Maybe if I could be trusted with baby ducks, I might someday graduate to making a difference in actual human lives! What a concept.

The very next spring, I was heading to a tennis match with a rare extra ten minutes to spare. A petite, elderly birdlike woman had stopped her car across two lanes of traffic and was waving her arms frantically. I got out and saw nearly the identical ugly scene playing out: At least ten baby ducklings who could barely walk on their giant flippers were tumbling one by one into the two-inch grates in a storm drain at the side of the road. The woman was emotionally overwrought, calling the Humane Society, the police, anyone she could think of for help. Never one to miss an opportunity to overreact emotionally, I experienced a surreal new clearheaded calm as I lifted the heavy iron grate off the gutter, used a magazine from my car to block the outflow, and one by one lifted the flapping, flustered ducklings up to the sidewalk, where their mother quacked frantically. They were all safely headed off to the nearby waterway before the birdwoman even got off the phone and noticed I was there, and the emergency was over. She looked at me as if she'd seen a ghost.

Again, I felt such overwhelming joy and connection to God, like a little kid showing off new skills. Maybe it's one of those "You had to be there" moments, but what the heck—it was huge to me. My cup runneth over. And God played tennis with me that day, too, just flowing with his grace and supernatural energy; we could do no wrong, beating opponents who were *way* better than we were. These experiences connected me in thrilling leaps of my imagination, to my long-lost, beloved aunt Rosie, birdwoman of the Italian Alps, and to the heart-expanding beauty we find in nature, and why not give a shout-out to my own firstborn baby duckling up there at University of Oregon—"*Go Ducks!*"—and of course, always back to God. In fleeting moments like those, I could almost tangibly feel the hardness in my heart just melting so sweetly. As I saw God's providence for even the smallest creatures in his creation, it helped me to see more clearly the countless ways he provides for my every need, and in that place of gratitude, I could rest from my incessant tendency to worry . . . and that being released, the seeds of contentment and joy have a fighting chance to bloom and grow.

# Happy Birthday, Dear Rose!

*A letter to my friend Rose on her birthday:*

In honor of your glorious birth, I wanted to share with you a strange vision that I treasure from about ten years ago . . . I awoke in the middle of the night and saw a bright light in the shape of a rose on the wall at the end of my bed. I rubbed by eyes and blinked hard to make sure I wasn't dreaming or imagining it. It kind of freaked me out, so I did some reading the next day and found that the rose is considered a symbol of Christ . . . with its thorns and its extraordinary beauty. I just wanted to make sure you knew that about your name, so that you can claim its beauty and strength and promise. I have not told that story to many people because it is so strange, but I am grateful for that elegant reminder of God watching over me as I sleep. When I was little, my grammy told me my name, Elizabeth, means "God is her oath," and that imprinted *huge* on my child's imagination. I am certain it set me on this faith quest.

When I was growing up, we didn't have many luxuries, but my dad had the sweetest tradition of giving me a single red rose for my birthday. Many years later when Roger and I got married that same month as my birthday, Dad slipped my new husband a few bucks, asking him to make sure I got that rose while we were on our honeymoon. The memory chokes me up to this day.

One last rose story: When my beloved dog Sky died, I just went into a pit of despair. So many sweet people rallied around with their sympathy and encouragement. An unexpected gift arrived on my doorstep from my neighbor Tracey, who had been shopping at Costco and had impulsively purchased a dozen pink roses and left them on my porch. It was a scorching day, and they were looking droopy.

I didn't mention how the heat on the porch had zapped them when I called to thank her. She said, "Oh, Costco has the best roses!" I put them in water and watched them hold up almost supernaturally for nearly three weeks, reminding me that Christ was up to something beautiful and mysterious in this sad, underwater place I was in . . . and when they finally drooped their heads, one in the center held fast, perfectly petrified, making sure I noticed, that Jesus was there, in the center of *everything,* defying nature, blessing even sadness with beauty and hope . . . and when I told this story to my neighbor who always kind of thought I was a little too "religious," I could tell that she received it and was touched by this sentimental gardener-God who was looking out for my heart.

# Practicing Counseling Without a License

*A preachy, long-winded letter to a friend stuck in depression:*

I have been thinking of our walk and our talk this morning, and so many unsaid thoughts keep popping up for me that I had to attempt to capture them here on paper while they are freshly hatched. I hope you are journaling right now, too, because in that daring act of self-examination and reflection, real wisdom has a fighting chance to shine through, when we are bold enough to give it space to take flight. Never apologize for your feelings . . . they can be scary, but we need to see them for what they truly are and not be afraid of them—and not be skittish and run away from them like so many people regularly do, self-medicating with alcohol or food or shopping or hyperactive social lives or a thousand other detours/distractions. Our feelings are here for a reason: to teach us something and help us change and evolve. If we wrestle with them, then we can move on and not get stuck in them or allow them to lie to us and make us heartsick . . . because when we wallow in them or get stuck in "disgusting self-pity," as a wise person once said to me, we only shoot ourselves in the foot.

As I see it, there are two major forces that play off each other in this life that no one around here talks about, but it is naive not to acknowledge the obvious, and we need to constantly, consciously, proactively *choose* one or the other: the good or the opposite of that, keeping watch, paying attention, and steering our ship toward the light instead of the darkness. In my vocabulary, it is God versus—as they say in the Harry Potter books—"He-Who-Shall-Not-Be-Named." Call it love or hate, whatever floats your boat—just do not take the bait and let the dark side torpedo your beautiful ship. My mantra for years has been "Never give up, never give up" because life really *is* hard, and we sensitive types feel *every* insult like a dagger in the heart . . . I thank you for your candor this morning, because it showed me a survivor's instinct in myself that I am prone to discount. We all have that tendency to rehearse and replay our struggles, remember every insult instead of counting our blessings—and they are legion—truly an embarrassment of riches.

I do not know what your experience is with spirituality, but I can guess that like so many people who grew up in the Midwest, you have been clubbed over the head with a Bible by wacky religious zealots, who have repelled you. You would not want to be in a club that would have them as a member . . . I so get that. I guess I just want to challenge you to think about it differently in the next three weeks as you purpose to reprogram your thinking, as you dare yourself to re-envision the way you do life, to reframe your struggles as growth opportunities, to bless and honor that exquisite sensitivity in yourself that makes you feel your feelings so vividly that you cannot and will not bluff or hide . . . that beautiful honesty and humanness that is the polar opposite of the fake "happy all the time" mentality that we see all around us . . . that is a lie.

You are real and true. I do like the idea of snapping a rubber band on your wrist every time a negative thought pops into your head . . . a literal "snap" to help you train yourself to snap out of your pattern of thinking. And may a light bulb go on in your head every time you say the "D-word" (for depression) to yourself. Do not give it too much credence. Counteract it with something positive that you want to bloom and grow in yourself; actively replace it with hope-filled words like *joy, love, peace, gratitude* instead . . . whatever resonates for you. Start rehearsing what your highest best self might look like instead of defining yourself as a failure, a disappointment, the world's worst mother (my personal favorites!). A new favorite mantra of mine goes: "Do not take the bait, do not take the bait" because I am trying develop the eyes to recognize the work of the author of hate, the mocker of every good thing in this world, who is practiced at keeping us in crippling bondage to our fears and failures and regrets, who sets little traps up for us along our daily paths that can keep us distracted from God's true beautiful path. And I can honestly say that since investing in my faith walk, much of my heart and mind and spirit operates more in a heavenly economy now rather than the world's economy.

I do not look to other people for affirmation so much as for God's affirmation. I try to forgive the people who hurt me immediately, because I am too weak to carry it, because I so clearly see how sick it makes *me* to hold on to unforgiveness. And because I need so much forgiveness on a daily basis, I get that I also must dole out forgiveness lavishly so I can receive it properly in return—the old "What goes around comes around" deal. One of my favorite holy scriptures is "God's strength is made perfect in my weakness" . . . because it says to me that you are admitting that you are at the end of yourself and are at the exact point where you throw up your hands and can say "I am done/I have run out of answers, but I think I know someone who may have the answers, and I welcome *his* help." I am not interested in pretending or bluffing anymore. I always need help. I need people and intimacy, and I need God to be my quarterback, to drive the bus for me so I can just enjoy the ride. It is the most powerful place you can be. It is not one bit scary. If you are not comfortable making a leap of faith, just try taking a few baby steps in the general direction of God, toward light and love, and see if he doesn't more than meet you there. As the Good Book says: "Taste and see that the Lord is good."

I heard a teacher describe it recently like this, and I just loved it. God is like the sun, and the earth orbits around him . . . Jesus is like the light that emanates from the sun and shows us the way to live . . . and the Holy Spirit is like the warmth that the sunlight brings into our lives, bringing us wisdom and comfort and wise counsel. Isn't that beautiful? That is the kind of faith I cannot live without. People are bound to disappoint us because we are all ultimately colossally self-absorbed. But when we allow God's light and levity into the equation, his grace truly amazes and trumps everything.

Sorry, I am really getting preachy here . . . I just would feel stingy not sharing this part of my heart with you after our wonderful morning together. It is one of the magical mysteries of the universe that is far too underutilized in our modern world of competence and ûberefficiency and independence. They have all become red-flag words to me now. I think God wired us up to be dependent on each other and on him to be truly happy, and time and time again, I have seen him use our messiness to create holiness. It is all very counterintuitive and mysterious. Dare to take the wild ride of faith and make a practiced habit of chronicling and holding on to all the good, the sacred moments. The reality is, life is never as you picture it, but if you stay out of the way and let it unfold according to God's will and not our own stubborn human fumbling, life can be way better than we could ever have pictured it with our limited mortal imaginations.

Final thought and I will shut up. In this brave new year ahead, I just really want to try to be a grown-up and not a selfish, shallow adolescent, like the ones I live with now who start the day grumbling, and it deteriorates from there. I do not want to be a mean girl or a gossip or someone who perpetuates hate or negative emotions. We can and *will* and should do better than that. Let's make a concerted effort to love the people God places in our paths for who they are, for what they are capable of being, and let's try to pump our own selves up to make the changes we know we need to make to be happy, to be true to ourselves, because the only person we have a prayer of changing *is* our own self; the rest is futile. (I love that definition of insanity: doing the same thing over and over again and expecting a different result!) I am predicting that when we become that comfortable in our own skins, the inspirational ripple effect that goes out from there will be contagious and potentially world changing. Let's make sure we are not striving to be anything that we are not wired up to be . . . that we are living up to the unique God-ordained place in this world for one you, one me, etc. The world would be so boring and potentially hazardous if we were a bunch of clones or copycats. I have a kind of ADD-brain, where I am pretty overstimulated by life much of the time and need to withdraw, and write, and try to make sense of and simplify things, and I think sometimes people think I am aloof or passive about connecting. I hope you can see that it's not personal, that I love the spontaneous times we grab for each other; it is just a limited capacity in my brain wiring that makes me *me*.

Let's all try harder to be good students of what *each* of us really needs to be our personal best and make extra sure those needs are met because if we do not do that, no one else can or should. One of my favorite questions for moms is "What makes you happy?" If I ban the answer "When my family is happy," you cannot *believe* how many gals are stymied. Make a list of what you need to get a natural high, to feel nurtured, and schedule it in and make it *happen* . . . There is a *huge* disconnect that happens in the lives of women who are so good at pouring themselves out for other people and so *lousy* at paying attention to their own very real needs. My own mom left me the example of pouring herself out, literally to death, when she died of a heart attack at age forty-eight, while moving her last born into his college dorm . . . How's that for a remedy to the empty nest? And I still cannot get over that mother of four teenagers from Ross who jumped off the Golden Gate Bridge last year rather than reach out and admit things were not perfect and ask for help and support. You are so good at knowing what you need: a hug, an apology, a kind word of encouragement. Make sure you can really *receive* it, and take it in, and then fan the sparks and flames of all the good in yourself. Dare yourself to make a list of it so you can see it, and if it's hard for you, let your friends help you make it. Make sure you listen along the way to the whispers in your heart and mind and spirit because that is none other than the voice of God, encouraging and romancing you and drawing you close. The litmus test of any challenge that comes should always be, is this from God (the good guy?) or that other negative spirit? My prayer for you is that you stay in the light. I love these thoughts from Rick Warren's book *The Purpose Driven Life*:

> Be careful how you think; your life is shaped by your thoughts. Proverbs 4:23 (TEV)
>
> To change your life, you must change the way you think. Behind everything you do is a thought. Every behavior is motivated by a belief, and every action is prompted by an attitude. God revealed this thousands of years before psychologists understood it. Imagine

riding in a speedboat on a lake with an automatic pilot set to go east. If you decide to reverse course and head west, you have two possible ways to change the boat's direction. One way is to grab the steering wheel and physically force it to head in the opposite direction from where the autopilot is programmed to go. By sheer willpower, you could overcome the autopilot, but you'd feel constant resistance. Your arms would eventually tire of the stress, you'd let go of the steering wheel, and the boat would instantly head back east, the way it was internally programmed. This is what happens when you try to change your life with willpower; you say, "I'll force myself to eat less . . . stop smoking . . . quit being disorganized and late." And, yes, willpower can produce short-term change, but it creates constant internal stress because you haven't dealt with the root cause. The change doesn't feel natural. Eventually you give up and go off the diet. There is a better and easier way: Change your autopilot; in other words, the way you think.

"Let God transform you into a new person by changing the way you think." (Romans 12:2 NLT).

Change always starts first in the mind. The way you think determines the way you feel, and the way you feel influences the way you act, which means "there must be a spiritual renewal of your thoughts and attitudes" (Ephesians 4:23 NLT). To be like Christ you must develop the mind of Christ. The New Testament calls this mental shift "repentance," which in Greek literally means "to change your mind." To repent means to change the way you think—about God, yourself, sin, other people, life, your future, and everything else, and you adopt Christ's outlook and perspective on life.*

---

* Rick Warren, *The Purpose Driven Life*, 1st ed. Zondervan, 2002, p. 181. Reprinted by permission from the author.

# Front-Row Seat at the Miracle Show

I have known my friend Grace for more than thirty years. She is part Native American and can really tell a story like the lost ancient art that it is. When she gets on a roll, she commands rapt attention from beginning to end and watching her do life has definitely made me want to pay attention and step up my walk with God. Grace found her faith in college when most of us are busy ditching our own and screwing up very willfully right and left. She would tell you that the closest person in the world to her was her brother, Luke who was an intense, rugged fisherman up in Kodiak, Alaska. He was also the one person she could count on to make her laugh harder than anyone. She once went out with her brother on one of his commercial fishing boat runs, and they were caught up in one of those Arctic storms, holding on with white knuckles the entire journey, praying to survive the constant bombardment of brutalizing swells, and thinking how cruel it would be for their parents to lose two children at the same time. When it was mercifully over, she asked Luke, who had been glued to the helm, guiding the boat for fourteen straight hours, if that had been a particularly bad storm, he nonchalantly replied, "No, it was pretty normal." After that, Grace prayed daily for his protection and that he would find his way to faith and that angels would accompany him on his dangerous missions and keep him safe. He once confided to her that he harbored a long-standing fear of dying at sea, and she was able to assure him with absolute conviction that would not be the case. She had him covered.

After she graduated from the University of California, Santa Barbara, she spent some time working in Calcutta with Mother Teresa and then went on to graduate school at a Christian college and got her counseling degree. She tells a funny story about sending what she thought was a fantastic book on the topic of faith that she thought her kindred spirit of a brother might enjoy, and he replied by signing her up for a subscription to *Penthouse* magazine. She had some explaining to do with her eagle-eyed roommates there at the Christian school every month when the mail came.

Grace's brother Luke can only be described as a rugged individual, the very definition of the word *maverick* before John McCain and Sarah Palin ran the word into the ground and made me want to never use it again. Oh well, such is my resolve. As the story goes, Luke was out on the water with his crew in his beloved sixty-foot boat on the coldest night then on record, estimated at forty degrees below zero, and they had all agreed that they had caught enough fish to justify heading back to land, a good two hours away. It was 2:00 a.m. on a foggy, moonless night. Suddenly, the boat listed to the right, and without any further warning, dove almost completely vertical, nose straight down in the water, tossing the crew overboard into the frigid waters. Luke had just enough time to dive into the cabin to try to eke out a Mayday distress call, just barely giving their approximate position before the onrushing water shut down all power and tossed the refrigerator up against the only exit for the cabin, trapping him inside as the water flooded in. All alone in the darkness with the water rising, he began to feel claustrophobic but was startled to notice as he looked down that he could see well enough to identify a submerged porthole that appeared to be his only hope of exit. He dove down to try to kick it in but had little leverage or power under the water. Swimming up to catch what little air remained, he tried again, and again . . . never really having time to marvel at the bizarre fact that there was in fact light by which to see anything at all. At the time he was just surging in that adrenaline rush of instinctive survival.

Luke later confided that if he could have gotten to his gun, he would have shot himself, rather than face his dreaded fear of drowning at sea. When finally the water in the cabin was up to the last three inches of air, he took one last gulp to dive down to try to open the porthole one last time, and this time it popped out from the advancing water pressure just as he approached it, and he was able to swim through it with such ease that he later described it as feeling as nimble as a fish. And he was never too cold or disoriented as he swam, because the strange light source was still with him, as he swam up, up, up, so much farther than he thought was possible to hold his breath. When he surfaced, he met his crew, flailing about in an aimless panic without their fearless leader, trying to inflate the lifeboat. Together they righted the lifeboat and climbed in, and only then began feeling the hideous impact finally of just how cold they really were.

One of the men in the boat started to pray, but it began to get on Luke's nerves, because to him that meant they were going to die, so he banned the practice. Huddled together, hypothermia began to set in with its accompanying seductive temptation to give in to sleep, and then death. Incredibly, within five minutes another boat, aptly named the *Polar Star*, appeared out of nowhere, having heard the brief, aborted distress call with nothing but the sketchiest of details, and rescued them. The men were hoisted in a heap onto the deck like so many doomed fish. None could even walk. Survival protocol dictated stripping down buck naked, and huddling together for maximum warmth, which they all did, but being manly men, they would have preferred that little detail be gracefully omitted. All crew members were admitted to the hospital two hours later with hypothermia and ultimately survived the nightmarish ordeal. They all stayed in the hospital overnight except Luke, who went straight home to his wife and one-year-old daughter, his extraordinary life spared for another eighteen years before losing a long, cruel battle with cancer.

Luke got right back out on the sea soon after that, naming his new boat *Deliverance*, "after the movie," he said. Grace had a beautiful rough wooden cross made and sent to her brother, and in the center was this daring inscription: "Deliverance . . . bless this boat, to the One who brings true deliverance." She had every reason to expect her gift to be dismissed as some kind of newfangled boomerang to be tossed overboard at the first available opportunity, but she was grateful to hear from Luke's wife that he had in fact pounded it in firmly with nails into a prominent place on the deck, where it could be missed by no one, and from that day on, he had a practiced ritual of pressing his hand to it upon heading out to sea.

When Grace and I talk about faith and hope and love, we inevitably get inspired by the wildness and the daring we find in our adventures with God. We marvel at the lies and distortions that manage to put God's epic story into so small a box. The God we know and love is the instigator of the best stories ever told, the greatest adventures ever lived, the author of the most radical stands for justice, the romance broker of the most devastatingly beautiful love stories, the miracle worker offering us free front-row seats at his traveling miracle show. Somehow our culture has reduced this down to a set of rules and regulations that constrict our freedom instead of a healthy set of boundaries that guard our hearts and guarantee that we will be truly, radically free.

Faith, if we are doing it right, is the ultimate high, not just another thing on our crazy to-do lists. It is the thing that finesses and blesses our to-do lists if we must see it that way. We are far better off if we are able to let go of being control freaks and let God become the custodian of our eyes, ears, mind, and spirit—the guardian of our mouths (this last one has gotten me into so much trouble all my life). By inviting him to walk alongside us, he becomes the ultimate tour guide in life's safari, that supreme docent walking us through the museum, so nothing is lost on us. God's essence has been mistakenly framed primarily as judge, when the experience of him for me has been that of romancer and creative genius, encouraging me to be more childlike and playful rather than busy and dutiful and perfectionistic. Walking with him is not this rigid, complex set of rules but this beautiful perfume, like music that envelops you and inspires you and fuels you, distracting you in the sweetest ways, as close as each breath, as natural as your heartbeat, as intimate as a heartthrob, captivating thoughts and actions.

Following in the brilliant footsteps of Jesus Christ is indeed radical, even revolutionary. The very mention of his name seems to strike fear in the heart of our politically correct world, which seems to value tolerance even more than truth. We exist these days in shades of gray, sometimes vaguely, usually sincerely, aiming for a good life, and then getting exhausted with the effort, so often blowing it, and having to start over again, and again, and again. Ultimately if we are brave enough to surrender, we can relax into the arms of a tender God, who loves us like the perfect parent, promising us that his mercies are new every day.

I love this quote from one of my favorite books, *Blue Like Jazz: Nonreligious Thoughts on Christian Spirituality*, by Don Miller:

> I used to not like jazz music because jazz music doesn't resolve. But I was outside the Bagdad Theater in Portland one night when I saw a man playing the saxophone. I stood there for fifteen minutes, and he never opened his eyes.
>
> After that I liked jazz music.
>
> Sometimes you have to watch somebody love something before you can love it for yourself. It is as if they are showing you the way.
>
> I used to not like God because God didn't resolve. But that was before any of this happened.*

* Don Miller, *Blue Like Jazz: Nonreligious Thoughts on Christian Spirituality*, 1st Ed., Nelson, 2003, p. vii.

# It *Is* a Wonderful Life

Recently I had lunch with a wise person who never has found the right person to do life with but remains ever hopeful, and he reminded me of a quote from the 2004 movie *Shall We Dance?* It was such sweet wisdom from such an unexpected source, one of those valentine-from-God moments, that I had to pass it on:

> Beverly (Susan Sarandon): "Why is it, do you think, that people get married? . . . Because we need a witness to our lives. There's a billion people on the planet. I mean, what does any one life really mean? But in a marriage, you're promising to care about everything—the good things, the bad things, the terrible things, the mundane things. All of it. All the time, every day. You're saying, 'Your life will not go unnoticed, because I will notice it. Your life will not go unwitnessed, because I will be your witness.'"

After all these years of loving my husband to the best of my limited ability, I am always searching for role models to inspire me when I get flat. Fortunately, I do not have to look further than my own in-laws' sixty-plus years of lasting true love. When they celebrated their fiftieth anniversary, we all wrote them a love letter with our favorite memories. This was mine:

> How to begin to put into words what your fifty years of marriage has meant to me? You two modeled the loyalty, commitment, and unconditional love that has now launched four very happy families and has truly inspired everyone in your circle of friends and extended family. You steered Roger and me to one of the key building blocks in the foundation of our marriage by arranging for us to meet with Father Lesley Wilder, who gave us a message that has been such a blessing and an inspiration: "Life is made up of many sacraments . . . the sacrament of Communion, the sacrament of baptism, the sacrament of marriage . . . but one of the most important and easiest to overlook is the sacrament of the moment. Remember it and keep it holy." I think of those words all the time, and it feels good to carve out a few moments now to enjoy the pictures of you two that flash through my mind.
>
> Sally, your reverence for the above sacraments may be best memorialized in your awesome quilting. I still marvel that you produced such wondrous works of art to commemorate each wedding and the birth of each grandchild. Each quilt, like each marriage and each child, a labor of love. How better to proclaim great love than with great art? Our wedding quilt especially reflects for me that wonderful quote from Anne Morrow Lindbergh's *A Gift from the Sea:*
>
> "Patience, patience, patience. That's what the sea teaches. Patience and faith."* I salute you for the creativity and love and focus that made each quilt and for the literal and symbolic warmth and protection each one brings. You have shared so generously with each of us in your gift for home decorating and hospitality . . . making every holiday and every birthday so wildly memorable, and

* Anne Morrow Lindbergh, *Gift From The Sea,* New York: Pantheon Books, 1955, p.17.

it plays *huge* in our children's imaginations. Thank you.

You two are so solid that we can always count on you to be our port in a storm. The way you stepped in on a moment's notice to take the kids when we needed to go to Seattle for Gary's funeral this year . . . and you did the same for their wedding. You have been our safety net . . . in good times and in bad . . . a sanctuary and a sacrament.

So many funny moments . . . the day Roger III was born was one of my favorites. The way my sister tells the story, she panicked outside the operating room when she heard the call for "more doctors in here, *stat*!" and her heart feared the worst, but you were fairly calm knowing it was more likely that extra gurney was for your highly evolved, em(pathetic) son . . . and of course never to be outdone in the drama department, the way Sally's protective instinct went after my blasé doctors who wanted to send me home from the hospital (this is "false" labor) on the day we both knew Lucy would arrive . . . the moment you placed your hand on my gigantic belly triggering that tsunami contraction that broke my water and announced to the skeptics that we meant business . . . you and Lucy and I are all good party girls by nature, and we had Rog Sr.'s birthday party to make that next Saturday! Those two amazing baptismal sacraments in your garden are such treasured memories. And I love that both our kids get to share a birthday party with each grandparent . . . such sweet symmetry . . . Roger III is the boy Sally just knew would come to continue the Rog dynasty, and we get to celebrate together that first week in August . . . Then in October it's the Rog Sr. and Lucy show. Lucy is so crazy about her Papa . . . his words of encouragement, his easy way of laughing with her and at her makes her glow with a special affinity . . . at last someone who really "gets her act" and appreciates her wacky individuality . . . her hero. Truly, Roger, I salute you for being the most positive, encouraging, thoughtful person who has ever graced my life . . . and I am so blessed to be a part of your family. Wow. You, too, reflect that beautiful gift from the sea (no small feat for a boy from Iowa!) . . . patience and faith. You light up our world with your laughter and kindness, and you have been the greatest role model for your four wonderful sons. You have been so generous with us in every way, and it gives us all such a thrill to look forward to being as free and as playful and joyful as you two are right now . . . globe-trotting and celebrating life and the fruits of your labors of love together. May God continue to bless you and keep you healthy and hold you closely in the palm of his hand.

Happy fiftieth anniversary . . . and many more. With great love and respect always,

Liz

P.S. They ultimately made it to an almost unheard of seventy-two years of marriage.

We all really *need* people to show us how it's done, and I honestly think it is getting harder and harder to find great examples of enduring, thriving, highly evolved marriages anymore. We are selfish, fainthearted creatures who give up far too easily. I know for sure that lasting love has a lot to do with humor and lavish forgiveness, celebrating our differences . . . different perspectives and skill sets can all add up to a complementary *team.* And let's face it: We would all go insane or die of boredom if we married ourselves. The more we know a person, the more aware we are of weaknesses, habits, personality traits that, like magnets, can attract and repel. It is so key to remember who it was you fell in love with originally as well as who you held yourself out to be as a sweet young thing. In our human laziness, we are so prone to point fingers and assign blame rather than catch our mate at their best self, doing good and respecting and fanning those flames instead. It's like that ancient biblical conundrum: "What splinter am I trying to remove from your eye that I cannot quite get to because of the log stuck in my own eye?"

I find it helpful when something or someone triggers a strong negative reaction in me to turn that mirror on myself and really ponder honestly *why* that pushes my buttons so fiercely, and to try to work on my own personality/character flaws through that filter, since that's really the only thing I have control over anyway . . . so help me God. It is so our human nature to keep a record of wrongs, so countercultural, counterintuitive to practice cataloging and focusing on good things and blessings. I know for sure I have been criminally stingy with kind words to my loved ones. As my faith life evolves and ferments, I am seeing more and more that forgiveness and gratitude are key to love. When we begin to grasp how *much* we have been forgiven in this life and stand in awe of that for a moment, it becomes more and more natural to forgive others freely . . . and in that environment I think deep, enduring love has its best chance to bloom and grow and evolve. The man I fell in love with all those years ago was brilliant at using "the art of the pump," which was a game he naturally played with his "fellers" from college:

"Hey, pal, have you been working out?"

"Oh no, pal, these muscles are nothing compared to your guns there . . ."

"*No*! I mean it, you've always been the athletic one . . ." And they would pump each other up and up, then the next guy would try to top that, and it could go around and around until the game would finally end with someone making an aside, "He totally bought it!"

The beautiful things that my husband says behind my back have a way of getting back to me and just melting my heart again and again. He is my champion, my most faithful love slave, and so worthy of my honor and respect. And I just *love* that he is legally blind without his contact lenses, so when the lights go down, he still sees the gal he married after all these years.

So why do you think I bit his head off when he dared to suggest that I owed my son an apology for dumping guilt on his head, for keeping me up waiting for him until 3:00 a.m. the night before, effectively sabotaging our planned one-night getaway for our twenty-year anniversary? I guess I wanted to shake things up with our son and make him feel the pain and frustration I had been feeling in my dreaded new role of prison warden/curfew enforcer/doormat for my darling boy who thought I should really just take a sleeping pill and get over myself. But in the global perspective, my husband was right; heaping guilt is manipulative and is so not from God, and I was wickedly shrill and angry . . . modeling exactly the kind of behavior I did *not* want to see flipped back at me by a seventeen-year-old, who was loath to say the simple disarming words "I'm sorry." (I do *not* know where he got that!)

One thing I knew for sure: Teenagers play parents off each other brilliantly, and it is important to be a united front. My husband's criticism, meant to be constructive, still made me furious, and I have never learned to fight, fair or otherwise. Nevertheless, I marched upstairs with a bad attitude and apologized to my son for the guilt and my theatrics . . . calmly trying to explain how *very much* I needed a romantic night off with no drama. And I didn't really get around to saying I was sorry to my husband, so I will say it here for the record. I do not know how you do it, Sweetie. It must be exhausting to be married to me. I hope it is all worth it for you. Truth be told, drama is kind of my normal. I am getting more comfortable with grief, and my life is full of laughter and humor . . . it's the in-between stuff that is a challenge for me. Normal kind of loses me. I live a life that looks pretty good on paper, but the way I love the people in my life sometimes seems more of a head concept than a heart action. That is my challenge with God too . . . getting it out of my head to piercing and changing my heart and really experiencing his extravagant, life-transforming love so that it can then melt my rough edges and radiate out to others.

I think ultimately my pride gets in the way. I was raised in the confused era between the domestic bliss of the 1950s and the radical rebellion of the '60s, to be a good girl, where children were seen and not heard from too much, when all around me just seemed to be absolute chaos. The hideous assassinations of JFK, MLK, RFK; the civil rights mayhem; the Vietnam war; and the Charles Manson murders that happened an hour away from our home were such awful things for a child's mind to know where to file politely away. I spent many sleepless nights anticipating the atomic bomb going off, and my bedroom was ground zero. I got pretty good at pretending, living in a parallel universe of my own imaginings, where I was safe, invisible even, no trouble at all . . . but I was really never young. So often I didn't speak, to keep the peace, and I think I now have this simmering, festering resentment with authority figures that I need to unlearn, because if I do not, I am doomed to watch history repeat and repeat with my feisty, fiercely independent children. Independence, I believe, is a highly overrated virtue in our culture, probably literally dating back to the Declaration of Independence. It is hard for us to find the liberation of surrendering our gigantic egos to something greater than ourselves. That tension is everywhere—"from the mountains to the prairies, to the oceans, white with foam . . . God bless America!" We need to figure out how to work together, in communities and families, and be more comfortable linking arms to do life together rather than in our little isolation pods of independence.

My children's generation came of age with the horrors of the school shootings in Columbine, Sandy Hook, and their copycats, and of course 9/11 . . . and I wonder if they ever felt really safe, if they ever got to feel the pure freedom of getting on an airplane headed for adventure, not preoccupied with terrorist hijackings or being patted down by airport security. And I guess my mother's and grandmothers' generations had the Great Wars and the Depression to carve up their character . . . indeed, it's always something.

As embarrassing as it is to admit, the old high school cheerleading days were good training for domestic life. We have got to be good encouragers, be each other's biggest fans. We have got to be good students of our loved ones' love languages. For me, I am guaranteed the most beautiful night's sleep if my husband remembers to stroke my hair and/or back and shoulders as I wind down and drift off. All I really need to do to thrill him is to make two or more fresh vegetables for dinner for his new health kick. And for my son, it was cooking a lot of meat, and then for my daughter, it was her new vegan diet. So on goes the schizophrenic circus, but just paying attention really to what rocks your loved ones' world is *huge*. It is also paying attention to feeding yourself the good things your soul needs, because no one else really can.

I think many marriages can fall apart on that false romantic notion from the *Jerry Maguire* movie, "You complete me," when really only God can do that. We gals really can get derailed by pouring ourselves out to distraction, and sometimes we really need to keep a short list of "What gets you high?" for when the going gets tough, to recharge our batteries organically. For me, what works are a good book, a soak in the bathtub, church on Sundays, the amazing enduring sisterhood of my girlfriends who aren't afraid to go deep, inspired music, always fresh air—a walk on the beach or a hike in the hills, preferably with my faithful dog Sky—and time with God. These are all tried and true remedies that get me back to center so that I have something to give out again to others. I need to proactively build in margins so I can keep dreaming *big* dreams and feeding creativity.

Our twentieth anniversary was nothing like what I had pictured it to be. Our son had been on academic probation since a regrettable choice he made on Saint Patrick's Day, involving a Guinness beer on his lunch hour, consumed just off campus. In my heart I know he had been stressed out, trying to graduate, appeal his rejected application to University of Oregon, and finish his Eagle Scout requirements, and he had organized an amazing memorial concert honoring his friend who had jumped off the Golden Gate Bridge a month prior. I know for sure he was struggling with where he could possibly file that memory away. His friends had cut their last classes after that lunch, but Eagle Scout boy went back for his last class, and it was painfully obvious to all that he was intoxicated. His personality was changed to the point that I didn't recognize him. As part of his punishment, he would have to be perfect for the last months of school and would then need to appeal the right to walk in the graduation ceremonies. Ever the optimist, he went into the appeal process sort of flying by the seat of his pants, and just *bombed* in his answers. He became immediately defensive and kept repeating and repeating the same vague explanation and never quite apologized, and was rejected, three days before graduation. The next day was our twentieth anniversary. I stormed into the principal's office, delivering this letter:

Dear Principal,

We strongly do not condone what our son did and agree that he alone is responsible for being in this situation in the first place. We are not sweeping his actions under the rug or asking for special treatment. The reason we asked to see you today is that we feel the policy set forth for the appeal by your vice principal was not followed. We also want to voice our disappointment with the school's disability policy that we feel affects many students.

Your vice principal is very professional and talented in a very challenging job. We met with her and Roger, and she laid out a very specific agenda, saying, "Roger, if you want to walk at the graduation ceremony, here's what you must do." She then gave some very specific and very effective guidelines for what was expected from our son: alcohol counseling, psychological counseling for his anger, community service, no behavior incidences, and perfect attendance (including senior ditch day). She seemed pleased that we mentioned church counseling as well.

We submit that these guidelines (as well as our own additional punishments) were observed, and the desired results achieved, yet the appeal board was either unaware of or disregarded the fact that these guidelines had been set forth. The appeal board was instead focused on what happened on Saint Patrick's Day and not what has been accomplished in the interim.

Another issue that comes to bear is the way in which our school deals with ADD. From our experience, there is a policy of discouraging all but the most severe ADD kids from being classified as IEP or offering any resources. I am sure you know that ADD kids suffer from impulsivity, low self-esteem, laboring under a haunting inner voice telling them they are different, not quite as smart as everyone else. Your school does a brilliant job of cranking out A+ students but may inadvertently be telling many average students that they just can't cut it. ADD kids need to be set up for success and be caught doing something good.

A perfect example of this failed policy took place in the appeal board. You had our son, diagnosed with ADD and dyslexia, without any accommodation or advocacy, put in a position of trying to articulate his growth to a panel of five adults whose line of questioning was very severe. This is not only very unfair, but it also borders on unethical.

I want to repeat we do not for a minute excuse the behavior that put him before the appeal board. There are not many parents of teenagers that aren't fighting this battle with alcohol and drugs. We have circled the wagons around our son in as many creative ways as we can to drive home the lesson that underage drinking will not be tolerated and that it is a fast track to misery and failure. His impulsive choice to drink on Saint Patrick's Day was severely punished, and he is proud of how he has changed and remained clean and sober since that day, supported by a parade of counselors, extended church family, community role models, and mentors.

In closing let me highlight some things that illustrate the change we see in our son. Just yesterday, his dad, sister, and I went off to an all-day volleyball tournament in Oakland at 7:00 a.m. and later learned that he had gotten himself up and off to church for the 9:00 a.m. service, where he gave blood at the bloodmobile in the church parking lot and went home to raise $300 toward funding his Eagle Scout project, all of his own volition. You have got to admit that is pretty amazing use of a Sunday for a seventeen-year-old boy.

This is our son, and we are very proud of him, and we want to celebrate his successes at the graduation ceremonies. Not allowing him to walk at graduation is not only an injustice, but also cruel and unnecessary shaming for a young man and his extended family and loved ones.

—Roger and Elizabeth Krakow

It turned out that the principal had raised two sons herself and showed such rare and surprising understanding that she agreed to speak to him again first thing the next morning, to ask the questions in a different way so that he could think clearly and make the positive points he wanted to make. We sat around the dinner table that night and helped him outline what he wanted to say, starting with an authentic apology. At 7:10 a.m. the next morning, our anniversary, our son casually let me know that he had left his talking points in his buddy's car the night before. That meant that my husband had to dash south in traffic to get the notes, and I would fling breakfast and get the kids to the school parking lot, where we would all try to meet and go over the notes one more time for five minutes. At 7:27 the phone rang. It was my husband saying he had the notes, and he was on his way back, and could I please look out the front door?

I snapped, "What?! I am still flinging breakfast, and we're running late . . ."

My son hooked his arm around me and walked me to the door, where there was this adorable red Vespa with a wicker basket on the back, with a "Happy Anniversary" balloon on it—just like the scooter we rode on all over Italy on our honeymoon.

How the heck had he pulled that one off on such a crazy morning? Shut me up good. My son and I raced off to the principal's office, met up with husband and the notes with three minutes to spare, and just sat in the parking lot, spent and sweaty, sending up prayers to cover our delinquent son as he made his last stand. Then my husband and I plotted our anniversary getaway from reality on the red scooter. An hour later we got the call that our boy had successfully redeemed himself, that he was going to help set up chairs for graduation, that he was not going to go on the senior ditch day but would like to go with us to the beach later instead. It was all very romantic . . . just the three of us . . . and the scooter could only accommodate two.

We made it to graduation the next day, and thankfully we didn't have to uninvite the grandparents, aunts, uncles, and cousins. I couldn't help noticing there was an especially loud round of applause when they announced our boy's name, because even his peers had been rooting for him to walk in the ceremony, because he *was* someone who tried to be positive, to walk differently through those dicey four years, and had not been the textbook poster boy for bad behavior. He gave the principal a giant bear hug when he received his diploma. The joy we all felt that day was truly explosive . . . made all the sweeter for surviving the struggle. I ran into our principal later that day, and she said, "I got a lot of hugs today, but I think Roger's hug meant the most to me." She is just such an angel . . . may God bless her always. And cheers to our marriage: May the next twenty be far less exhausting than the past twenty years.

It is meant to be a wonderful life. I am always on the lookout for good examples of that and have been inspired recently by a love story so epic it is a little intimidating to attempt to paint its portrait with words—it was so counter to what our modern-day world values that it might appear to be a far-fetched, over-the-top remake of *It's a Wonderful Life*. Truth is stranger than fiction. But I tried to capture it . . . for the record . . . for the sacredness of their moment in time . . . for posterity. Because it was a miracle in motion, and I got to have a front-row seat to watch some of the beauty unfold right before my very eyes.

A little over fifty years ago, a dashing young man was finishing his studies at San Francisco State with aspirations to become a priest. Born in Panama, he was a gifted three-sport varsity athlete who was offered a chance to play with the New York Yankees, which he turned down because his family was his priority. He had the most beautiful soulful eyes set into olive skin and the best legs I had ever seen, and he was in his seventies when I met him.

One day in the school cafeteria, while he was minding his own business, a feisty blond eighteen-year-old Irish-Catholic beauty named Eileen set her gaze upon him and felt something fierce seize her heart. It didn't make any logical sense to her then because, in her late adolescent's vision of perfection, her ideal man was tall, blond, and built more like her adored big brother. But something rabid seized her, an arrow from Cupid, and she went after him with a kind of animal instinct, charming her way into his heart with warp speed.

The priesthood never stood a chance. Ed proposed within three weeks, so sure and true were their hearts. And as their dear friend Father Vin once observed, "Together their life has been a ministry, touching and inspiring more lives than he ever could have influenced in a traditional priesthood." The way that they love everyone who is blessed to cross their paths is truly to see the face of God, unconditionally loved, seen, and heard, and treasured.

The nutshell version is that together Ed and Eileen gave birth to six boys in rapid succession and managed to raise them in one of the wealthiest communities in the country on a teacher/coach's salary. Along the way they also adopted three foster boys and countless others who wanted to share in the force field of love that organically emanated from them. Together they made a formidable basketball team. I count myself so fortunate to be a part of their adopted family. It kind of reminds me of the way God woos us into his family and adopts us . . . I've just never quite seen it played out so brilliantly on this planet by mere mortals. They seem to walk by faith and not by sight, and in God's economy—showing us all that "a wing and a prayer" can take you anywhere you want to go.

After all these years together, it was a marvel to behold. It kind of reminded me of my faithful dog Sky, who at sixteen was legally deaf and blind, but every morning she chirped out of bed, virtually dancing down the sidewalk on our morning constitutional, never faltering, so knowing *the way*. Ed and Eileen got it like that. And I am hoping that if I hang around them long enough, some of that good stuff will be contagious enough to rub off on me. Imagine being married fifty-plus years and still being so sexy and flirty and funny and such a *team*.

To paint too perfect a picture is to undermine the beauty. Their challenges were fierce. When Ed and Eileen's second son Greg was eleven years old, he was hit by a drunk driver, pinning him against a wall, cutting off his leg. But they were quick to celebrate the fact that his was the first successful leg reattachment surgery, and they took such pride in watching him defy all odds as he came back to surpass the doctor's predictions that he might never quite even walk right again, joining his athletic brothers back on their basketball team. Later in life, that childhood assault triggered enough joint trauma that he conducted his life frozen into a wheelchair with rheumatoid arthritis, where he continued to keep up with three teenagers, coaching their teams, and inspiring all who knew him to bloom and grow where they were planted. He was one of my heroes in life. Last time we spoke, he was planning a development in Yosemite, where people with special needs could live in a beautiful, affordable home environment, with assistance, to enjoy a normal homey life where disabilities can be managed. He had more time than the average person to creatively brainstorm and solve the world's problems. He was a brilliant eternal optimist. My heart wanted to implode with the threat that the bank wanted to foreclose on his home, and yet he persevered.

His younger brother Buck owned the house with him. He was also a gifted coach and wonderful father of five young children. He loves his wife and children with a rare tenderness. He coached tennis and basketball at an elite private school and had such a beautiful way with teenagers that was so free and funny and brought out their very best. If a kid blew off practice, he would tell them that they "owed him a song," and it was such a wonder to watch these "too-cool-for-school" teenagers burst into some cornball show tune. Buck is all about fun and fairness and making the world a better place. He was also a lightning rod for controversy, because he did things like letting his second-string players play as much as his first stringers, even when they were losing because, guess what: Winning isn't everything. He is a passionate advocate for sports as a forum for building character, fun, and friendships instead of competition, pressure, and winning at all costs. It totally freaks people out. He is more fun than a barrel of monkeys to hang out with and a magnet for people. My favorite thing about Buck is his absolute detachment from money. When he was a young man, he played professional basketball in Mexico for a couple of years, where he was known for handing out all his money as he walked down the street to get breakfast or to practice. Recently he received a large check from an anonymous friend, and he had to open a checking account for the first time in his life, and he was outraged to learn that banks charge a $6.95 monthly service charge. It is difficult to imagine that he has been able to raise five kids in this affluent county without a checking account. He recently told me that the flu was running through his entire family and that they were all home together throwing up and fighting for the bathroom, and I thought I knew where he was going with the story, but then he said, "Oh, we had the most wonderful day together!" No school, no pressures—he so adores his wife and their children—and he naturally makes everyone he meets feel like they are the most important person in the world.

Buck can bring levity to any situation with the countercultural grace of his unique personality. He met regularly with our son in his junior and senior year for basketball and tennis lessons, but it was really for some of his magic "world-according-to-Buck" life lessons. They would meet after school for an hour, Buck sporting a rumpled Chevy's sombrero and usually paint-splattered pajama pants full of holes. Not quite the crisp typical tennis pro, but within minutes his charismatic personality would attract a gang of teenagers to cheerfully take him up on his dare to pick up ten pieces of trash from the school parking lot before playing. He would joke with them all the while, perhaps crooning a Frank Sinatra tune with his beautiful voice that always stops people in their tracks. For a cranky teenager to get to spend an hour in Buck's world was to be exposed to a kind of truth and beauty and gratitude and joy and whimsy and a love force field so magnetic and contagious it was positively world changing. It is too rare these days to see an adult speak the teenage love language so beautifully.

Buck is capable of finding the good in everything. A while ago, he found a lump in his leg, and they biopsied it, and he was told it was cancer and he needed surgery to remove it. After the surgery, the doctor came to him wringing his hands, apologetically telling him the biopsy had been misread and that it was in fact a very aggressive cancer, which would have indicated they amputate his leg.

Buck cheerfully reassured him, "Don't worry, Doc—I am sure it wasn't a mistake. God just didn't want you to remove my leg! I am an athlete and I need that leg!" The doctor was incredulous and insisted on monitoring him carefully for the ensuing years. Sadly, after seven years, the cancer reappeared, and again they were advising amputation but would not say that this would be a cure. So again, Buck stared down the diagnosis his way, refusing to dignify the cancer with too much energy. Wing and a prayer. If everyone who has loved him throughout his extraordinary life sends up a prayer, I have every reason to hope and expect another mountain can be moved. When Eileen told me the news, we were distraught, but we clearly, simply prayed, "Please, God, let us keep darling Buck." Buck and his brother Greg are shining testaments to Eileen and Ed's long love-filled marriage.

In all fairness, their marriage hasn't always been a lovefest. I remember a tennis lesson one day when Eileen arrived with visible steam coming out of her ears from one of those "Everything that could go wrong did go wrong" mornings. Throughout the tennis lesson, there was banter about Ed being in the doghouse. Later that day two of my teammates saw Ed at Safeway doing some redemptive grocery shopping for Eileen, and they were able to persuade the checker to announce on her microphone, "Ed Chavez, dog food on aisle nine." It became an ongoing joke at many team gatherings: a nicely wrapped can of dog food for Christmas or a can of dog food on a china plate at team banquets. Humor carried them through the inevitable bumps in the road. And the bumps keep coming. On New Year's Eve 2006, relentless rains produced a flash flood, bringing a four-foot wall of mud into their newly remodeled first floor, ruining their cars and countless family photos and keepsakes—and their insurance company continues to nickel-and-dime them for their losses. When I saw Eileen the next day, she was so sad and exhausted, but she made a point of playing for me a song Buck had left on her message machine, which brought her such joy: "Count Your Blessings (Instead of Sheep)."

A month later they were hit in broad daylight by a woman running a red light, totaling the new pickup truck they had just bought to replace their mud-filled one. They were badly bruised but appeared to have only suffered a broken wrist for Ed, but then two weeks later, he had a stroke. All though that tsunami, there was so much joy and laughter and a quiet confidence that this too shall pass, that amazing "peace that passes all understanding" that can only come from a faith that has been well-tested and has endured for a lifetime. People watch that and can't help but be inspired to try to cultivate that kind of "faith and hope and love . . . but the greatest of these is love" (1 Corinthians 13).

Marriage may be in danger of becoming a dinosaur in our culture of record-breaking divorce rates. It requires a leap of faith that scares people, or if it doesn't scare them, the leap may happen impulsively before they really know themselves. My own grandparents were married for more than sixty years, beginning with their stolen first date when my aunt Helen couldn't get off work one night and her younger sister, my grammie Ruthie, conspired to hop into the rumble seat with my future gramps instead . . . because he was such a sharp dresser and a fine dancer.

Maybe true love happens not so much in that leap of faith but in intentional baby steps aimed in the right general direction of love and God—the two words are synonymous to me now. It is so counter to the hedonistic values of our age, which urge us to do what feels good now, keeping our options open, looking out for number one. The truth is we find our happiness by giving it out to others, and if we stay out of its way, that loaves-and-fishes multiplying effect can kick in, and love can bloom and grow against all worldly odds. Just baby steps . . . and when you fall as all toddlers do, you pick yourself up and take the next right steps toward love. I watched my friend Carey fight so hard to save her marriage when it was threatened, but it is a very rare thing to witness anymore. I love that E. L. Doctorow quote that talks about how you can drive all night long seeing only the five feet in front of you illuminated by headlights; you do not have to see the whole road and can in fact make the whole journey that way. Trust those baby steps in the right direction. Be a love slave, president of each other's fan club.

Resting my head the other night on my husband's chest, I heard his heart beating and felt a little leap as my own aligned with his in harmonic resonance . . . "ah-*bah*, ah-*bah*." The sound connected me instantly to a crystal-clear old picture in my mind of our son in his highchair blowing slobbery dramatic kisses . . . ah-*bah*! And then my mind leaped again to the ancient affectionate word for God . . . Abba (Daddy) . . . and I drifted off so sweetly to sleep pondering that beautiful, bundled definition of love and God and messy kisses.

# Happy Birthdaze

An unexpected wave of fresh grief washed over me as I noticed the date. Today would have been my mom's sixty-eighth birthday. It had been so many years since I had seen her, and the shock of that realization made tears well up in my eyes. I was very quick to try to be macho about it all and write it off to that time of the month. Ever since reading *The Red Tent* earlier that year, I have had fond fantasies of a tent in the sand somewhere, a place where I could retreat with all my wayward hormones and not have to inflict myself on any unsuspecting souls . . . where I could just be my emotional self with a few gal pals who would not think I'm completely unredeemable.

It had been over a month since I'd had the luxury of sitting down to write a single word on this computer, unless you count the two impassioned letters to each of my children's school principals explaining their special needs and learning styles. I suppose it is no coincidence that day the house was quiet, and I could be still . . . I love the verse: "Be still and know that I am God." I have been so off-center that month, trying to wedge it all in under my own power, as we sprinted toward summer. It happened like clockwork every year about that time, and I do know better. It must be under God's power, or it is an exercise in futility. Our pastor, who was introduced that day as "the pastor currently known as Prince" went so far as to declare worry and fear as the spiritual equivalent of atheism. Radical truth. A further illustration on that theme would be that my lack of finding time to write is the equivalent of my lack of time for feeding my faith. When I can steal a moment to ponder my words on the page, I can get more of a God's-eye view of things, and it all began to make more sense. It was a time for meditation on all that I had to be grateful for and to try to process and forgive all my regrets.

I remember when a group of kids from our church's middle school youth group were planning to be baptized, and our son was excited to join in. He had spent three days on his Thanksgiving vacation with this group packaging Christmas care packages for needy kids, and they had really bonded. Unfortunately, the Boy Scouts were also going white water river rafting, which was cast in stone since Dad was now the new scout master (and I and my bad attitude, the new scout widow), which also meant that we had to call his baseball coach and let him know he would be missing the big game . . . a typical weekend for the Krakow family. Then the nicest thing happened. The Big Guy in charge of the weather sent torrential rains, and wouldn't you know they had to cancel the rafting trip for safety reasons. We took it as a sign that this baptism thing was meant to be.

The night before, I was talking to Rog about getting baptized, and I told him I was really impressed with him stepping out like that in a county where only 2 percent of the population even attends church regularly. I read recently that Marin County is a bigger mission field than China, where it is illegal to practice Christianity, and so of course in our reverse psychology world, it was growing there by leaps and bounds. I told him that I thought it was really courageous and cool to make this step. And then he said, "So why don't you do it with me? You were only baptized when you were a baby." It was just too sweet a dare to refuse. But I, too, had a problem. I had been operating under the presumption that I was going to be alone for the weekend, so I had signed up to play in a doubles tournament with a darling new Italian friend of mine, a beautiful tennis player, and I really didn't want to disappoint her.

So on the morning of the tournament and baptism, we started to play at 9:00, but by 9:30 this wimpy little rain began to make the courts slippery. We went inside, and within a half hour it was dry again. We played a few more games, and it all started up again. It was now 10:30, and I figured that in the best-case scenario, it would be another forty minutes before the courts could dry, and if I factored in my commute time back to church and, say, another hour to finish the match, I would be in serious danger of missing the 1:00 baptism. I decided that since God was in charge of the weather, I would just get on the road and trust them to reschedule the match later in the afternoon. Ten minutes down the road, my cell phone rang, calling me back to play or asking me to default. I felt so torn, not wanting to disappoint anyone, such an impossible way to try to do life. It was totally insane, but I wanted to try to keep my commitments, knowing that God is in charge, and fully capable of controlling the weather and making time stand still if need be. I know this sounds like I was totally wasting a request for a miracle on a tennis tournament, but it was more than that. I had this newfound confidence that God made me this way, to be someone who swings at every pitch, and he is more than a little concerned with my tendency to overcommit and drop balls right and left as a result. But I also had a sense that he loves my loyalty to the people in my life too, and this seemed like one of those leap-of-faith things in a way—that I needed to trust him to make order out of my messed-up day. So I asked God to run interference for me, and I asked for help to honor my commitments and promised that I would definitely default if it got to be twenty minutes to 1:00, guaranteeing I'd be late for the baptism, which was so clearly a priority. I can honestly tell you that the weather held beautifully, the match progressed like a well-choreographed dance, and we won in record time, and I got to the big event with minutes to spare.

I felt a little idiotic showing up in my tennis whites to such a sacred event, but when I got there, it was actually kind of perfect. I had attended these things before and had secretly agonized about what I would wear to a total immersion baptism, being more than a little self-conscious about the extra pounds hanging around my middle since having those two giant babies. So there I was, with a bunch of beautiful teenagers and their nubile young bodies in bathing suits, and what the heck else would I wear? It was drip-dry, discreet, sporty . . . my friend Grace said it was perfect. And guess what? It's not supposed to be about what you wear, dude. It's what's inside that counts. Radical.

The teenagers and I got to spend a few minutes with our pastor discussing the meaning of all this. The kids were all composed and lovely, and there was this weird geeky reverse vibe with me sort of apologizing for horning in on their event, and my son had to shoot me a look to shut me up. We talked about how there were two schools of thought about baptism: Is it something you do for God, or is it something God does for you? It is definitely a public statement of faith, of standing up for what you know is true and foundational and nonnegotiable in your life. If it might bring a smile to God's face, then what a joy to do it. But it was also infused with this huge hope, for me anyway, that it might be a mystical turning point in the life of my faith, where my fervent prayer that God might really change me, and do something good with my life, and maybe even nuke that dark rain cloud that hangs over my head . . . would really be answered. Dear God, let me see more of you and less of me. Might I actually get to see some of those fruits of the Holy Spirit—love, joy, peace, patience, kindness, goodness, thankfulness, gentleness, and self-control—begin to take root in my crazy life? *Gaacchk!* Still, God loves a project. It was a beautiful day and a very special memory . . . but the epiphany that I envisioned for it to be in my life failed to materialize in a big way.

The month that followed was accompanied by one of the worst brain fogs I have ever experienced. My moods were all over the place. I was getting calls from the kids' teachers, the family calendar was out of control, I was so exhausted I would try to pray and fall right to sleep. My friend Carol gave me the book *Too Busy Not to Pray*, which I was so excited to read that I promptly lost it somewhere in my exceedingly organized household. I attended a few meetings to collaborate on ways to help grow the church, all the while hoping I wouldn't volunteer to do anything significant to help since I would inevitably blow my assignment and feeling secretly like a hypocrite who really likes how small and cozy our church is. I tried to write but was so bored with myself I wanted to scream . . . not an original thought in my head. I felt so flat and uninspired and strangely distant from God. Also, I had given up coffee and alcoholic beverages cold turkey, joined Weight Watchers, and was probably expecting a few too many miracles for the one small month. Sometimes in my dreamer's mind, I can be such a simpleton with God, and our relationship is akin to that of Cinderella and her fairy godmother . . . just wanting him to wave his wand and make everything magically all right—with a Hollywood Technicolor flourish. Truth be told, he is every bit as attentive and indulgent as Cinderella's fairy godmother and has flooded my life with an embarrassment of riches. But God's ways are not our ways, and his grandeur and wisdom are something I can't expect my puny human brain to ever figure out. Sometimes his silences are more profound than his bolts of lightning. I look forward to spending the rest of this lifetime marveling at the way he works.

Growth and change are rarely fun and usually more like torture. After that long foggy month, one day I woke up and felt a strange new sensation of clarity and connection to God. Not only that, but my stomach also felt noticeably flatter, and when I weighed in at Weight Watchers, I had lost ten pounds. Wheee! And God reminded me that if that wasn't evidence of patience and self-control, he didn't know what was. So then I went to my Bible study, and my friend Debbie said that I had a great glow on my face and looked a little like Bo Derek. Ka-ching! And then my son, who hadn't had much to say to me, pumped me up with a compliment about how he had really noticed how involved I was in giving to other people at church, at school, on my tennis team, and in town projects and that he thought that was really good. So there we've got the love and joy fruits abounding, which allowed for peace to trickle in and mingle with the many kindnesses the people in my life were blessing me with, and I could begin to see that in all last month's fog and silence, there were plans in the works for my character. God whispered that I needn't be impatient with him for not transforming me into a holy person like Mother Teresa, or someone that I could actually respect . . . that he needed me to be me, the czarina of the mundane, that he was actually quite pleased with his creation and far more interested in growing my character than fixing my personality, although he could do with less of that negative banter I've always got looping through my head because frankly, it hurts *his* feelings! That strange dry spell also taught me a lot about the nature of faith: that often it is enough to just keep showing up and trusting God to unravel the tangled-up strings of your kite so you can fly again.

Quite a few years ago, my sister rented a beach house at Stinson, where we had the most perfect day, bodysurfing in that icy cold refreshing water, barbequing, and just having a glorious day of spontaneous family fun. We didn't want it to end. And so instead of driving back that night, we threw down sleeping bags and slept anywhere we could. I found the best spot, in a window seat tucked right into the dunes where I could hear the pounding surf all night long. It was so loud, I couldn't completely drift off to sleep, but it was so lovely looking out the window, it didn't much matter. Around midnight I was startled to full alertness by a sound that can only be described as a flutter of breeze blowing across the piano keys across the room from me. The dog, sleeping beside me, growled under her breath like something was really up here. There was no wind in the room at all, but the piano keys kept fluttering the most ethereal riffs. I pinched myself to make sure I wasn't dreaming or making any of this up. I wasn't afraid, but I had to admit something very strange was going on. And then it passed, as quickly as it had arrived, leaving me to make some explanation for myself. It didn't take me long to realize the significance: That perfect day we had all just spent together had been Mom's birthday . . . and quite unbeknownst to us, it had been exactly the kind of birthday party she would have wished for us to enjoy—on the beach, living it up good, oblivious to her—yet there she was, wanting to insert herself in there with a brief artistic flourish as the clock turned midnight to mark the moment. I still don't quite know what to make of that strange encounter, but I think it was the beginning of God calling me to be a rememberer, to pay attention and connect the dots along the path of life, and to treasure those moments that take your breath away for what they can teach us about perseverance, patience, and faith.

And so, in honor of my mother's birthday, I resolved to let go of that little bundle of sadness and grief I had been holding on to so tightly for so long, taking with me the beautiful gifts she left me to show me how to live a full and happy life. And as I stared down the barrel of the smoking gun of the decade that ended her life, I dared myself to rise above all that baggage and live the kind of life that could make a joyful noise here on planet Earth.

Birthdays are always a great opportunity for magic moments. One summer we had a great beach party celebrating Roy-tha-boy's entry into teenager-hood at Kirby Cove in the Golden Gate National Recreation area, with twenty-two or so of his close personal friends. Our campsite was nestled at the base of the Golden Gate Bridge, on a pristine strip of beach, which is hallowed ground for our family. I always loved hanging out with Roy's buddies, and they were great that day, frolicking in the surf, cooking their own hot dogs on sticks, making s'mores over the fire, and creating all their own easy fun. Five of them spent the night and were up pretty much all night long talking and laughing.

Just as I managed to grab some sleep, I was shaken awake by the jarring moaning and groaning of the fog horns, which must have been located somewhere in the trees of our campsite. They reverberate and no earplugs can contain their cacophony. It is a deep, haunting, longing noise that irritated something deep in my soul, prompting me to get up and check out the sunrise. I had to laugh when I went outside; there wasn't a hint of fog anywhere. Navigation technology has basically relegated the foghorns to dinosaur status, but I remember when they turned them off a while back, there was an outpouring of support for them to return just for the atmosphere and romance of the ancient tradition. Those people had obviously never tried to catch some sleep at our little campsite. Still, I was glad that I'd wrestled myself out of my sleeping bag to get to see this spectacular morning. I was exhausted and bleary-eyed, but I could look straight at the sun without it hurting my eyes . . . for a moment it was like being the only person alive, in my own perfect Garden of Eden, but as the sun rose in the sky, I had to avert my gaze because it was so brilliant. I closed my eyes and felt a strong sense of God painting this incredibly beautiful, peaceful picture of why he had to send Jesus to earth: to translate his brilliant holy essence that is really way too much for our mortal minds to comprehend . . . too blindingly bright for our eyes to even directly drink in . . . to be the Son/the Sun that solar-powers us. After two thousand years, the light of Jesus's life still lights our paths in countless ways and bridges the vast gap between God and man, heaven and earth . . . kind of like the way this amazing Golden Gate bridge stretches across the water, connecting me here in my nature perch to the jewel of San Francisco, and all of its worldly comforts and decadent trappings. It is an internationally recognized symbol of beauty and majesty, a testament to man's engineering genius to many—but also now for me it can morph into a gallows, which has been the site for thousands now to take their own lives into their hands and jump, two that I have known and want back. Beauty and pain, laughter and tears are inextricably entwined, informing each other.

Jesus's passionate life both inspires us and breaks our hearts, and he is literally our bridge to God and all his awesome glorious mysteries. In my Bible study, we have been looking at the way the Jews practiced animal sacrifices, because they understood the weight of their sin was so enormous that if they were to approach God in his perfect holiness, they could literally wilt in his presence. Through Christ's selfless act of laying down his life on the cross, he became the ultimate sacrifice to end all sacrifices . . . the bridge that made direct access to God a free gift for the asking . . . making true, fearless freedom accessible, graspable. It was a lovely postcard-from-heaven moment.

# Finances and Other Disasters

When I was growing up, we had just enough to get by. We lived by the beach, which was free, so that was all we needed to be happy. My elementary school was literally in the sand dunes of Pierpont Beach in Ventura. I remember noticing in junior high school that Janet Avediesian had more than one pair of shoes, and that was a caliber of wealth that pretty much blew my mind. I later went on to college and became an English major, so I consider myself uniquely qualified to dispense the following financial advice.

In 2008, the year the stock market crashed, the college fund that we had been saving for eighteen years was reduced to shreds at the exact time we needed to use it. It was tempting to despair, but God had not yet revealed some of his best juju. Rog-boy was accepted to the University of Oregon, which came with hefty out-of-state tuition, so we had to get creative and fast. We decided to start Airbnb-ing our house to make some extra income. We depended on the kindness of friends and neighbors to let us house-sit or crash in their guest bedrooms, or we would go camping, whenever we had a tenant. One day a woman inquired if she could rent the house more long-term, say six to nine months, while she was remodeling her home. She tried to negotiate a better deal on the rent, but we told her the only reason we were doing this was to fund our son's college tuition and we needed to keep our rates at top dollar. She took it anyway.

We moved into my old tennis coach's basement and voilà: Tuition was handled. Ten years later that tenant is still there. She loves our house better than her own. And the income from that venture enabled us to retire and travel and walk with a new confidence in God's economy. And gratefully, we are no longer in that basement: We found a darling, dumpy houseboat to fix up and have never looked back.

Three years later when Lucy was accepted to NYU, that Oregon tuition looked downright cheap. When I worried aloud about how we were going to afford that, Lucy leveled a crystal-clear gaze at me and said: "*Mom!* The hard part was getting into NYU. After that miracle, don't you think God will show us a way to pay for that too?" Indeed, she had talked herself into a very elite program, the Clive Davis School of Recorded Music, which only took ten or twelve kids a year. It shut me up good. To Lucy's credit, she graduated her darn self in three years, saving us $60,000 right there!

I will never forget the financial disaster we had when the bookkeeper at Roger's video editing company discovered that the manager that he had trusted to run the financial side of his creative business had embezzled more than $250,000. She had a perfect paper trail to prove the fraud, and we were brainstorming about how to proceed from there. This man had been a world-class schmoozer and had ingratiated himself to our kids, clients, you name it. Roger had always treated his employees like family and was absolutely blindsided. He was wrestling with the betrayal when Lucy, fresh out of Sunday school, overheard and said, "Dad. You have got to forgive him." Crazy as it sounds, it was the seeds of what eventually became a contract with the guilty party to pay back all the money in $2,500/month installments until all $250,000 was returned. There was a stipulation that if even one payment was missed, he agreed that he was guilty of the fraud and subject to prosecution. He never missed a payment. And those payments each month were pretty much exactly what the business needed to survive the postcrash economy in which many of Roger's competitors went out of business.

Wow.

Go, God, *go*! Wing and a prayer.

# Younger Next Year

My husband made me read a book called *Younger Next Year*. The premise is basically that our bodies are programmed to decay after fifty . . . the deal is you can fight back, one day at a time, with exercise. I find it very motivational to greet the day with the question "Do I feel like decaying more today, or should I get some exercise?" Even when I don't feel like it, the thought of decaying any further horrifies me into action.

I joined a tennis team and started to really enjoy the authentic sporty women I was meeting, and to my surprise, I loved the competition and the measurable increase in my strength and athleticism. Ten years ago, my partner, Amy Rennert, and I joined a new team in Golden Gate Park, all strangers to us, but we'd had a great undefeated year together so that got us recruited, following an audition with much younger gals that we had to impress with our crafty slicey-dicey game. It stretched us like nothing else. Amy played the deuce side, roaming the back court, virtually error-proof, setting me up at the net. I found that I did my best work on the ad-side, which forced me to hyperfocus on those clutch game-ending points. I was surprised to learn that when the going got tough, I actually wanted the pressure on me . . . a skill that would serve me well beyond the tennis court. My sister can't relate to my love for competing, but I tried to explain that it's not about vanquishing other women;

it is more about helping each other to be warriors, overcomers, stronger under the inevitable pressures of life.

My darling friend Lisa's husband, Frank, recently died of a sudden heart attack in his early fifties while she was away at our regional tennis championships. The shock of it slayed all of us who love their beautiful family. And I had never seen anyone grieve as hard as Lisa has. They were such a team and so in love. She would say with absolute conviction that her tennis community and close family saved her life and got her through that shock like nothing else could have.

My favorite book of that year was *The Boys in the Boat*. The coach spent countless hours analyzing team dynamics, trying to pinpoint just what combination it would take to go all the way to the national championships and the Olympics in Berlin. He knew it was not as simple as having the strongest people . . . it was more nuanced than that. Who was the hungriest? Whose heart was in it for the right reasons? Who brought out the best in each other? Who needed this the most? Who was seeking redemption, love, connection, the *family* experience it could become? Who was humble enough to know it wasn't about himself but for the good of the *team*, pulling for them, not the individual ego? Who thrived under pressure, welcomed it, used it to convert into adrenaline? Who had the fire and the composure and confidence? Who *believed* it was not a dream but potentially reality?

Our Golden Gate Park team believed. Ages twenties to sixties, we banded together and managed to win the eighteen and over national championships at the 4.0 level. It was all about the love . . . for our sport and for each other.

My other recent favorite book, *Find a Way* by Diana Nyad—which my tennis partner, Amy, championed as agent—speaks to the topic of encouraging women to tap into their superpowers after sixty. Diana Nyad's dream of swimming from Cuba to Florida haunted her as she attempted it several times in her twenties and thirties. It wasn't until she was in her sixties and still couldn't let go of that dream that she was able to show her younger self what she was made of and completed that nearly impossible feat.

Aging is such a privilege. It's so strange to think that I am so much older than my mother ever got to be. Lately there have been so many losses, but it is also a poignant reminder that there have been so darn many people that I got to love and will never really say goodbye to. We carry them onward and upward in our hearts and can talk to them anytime we want, because suddenly they are everywhere.

# Don't Let This Happen to You

My sister and I are fond of sneaking out in the early afternoon for a matinee. We love to sit in the cool, dark room and escape into someone else's life for a couple of hours and ideally gain some perspective on our own. Usually, we are cheapskates and smuggle in our own snacks. One recent afternoon when the lights went down, Mere pulled out a Coke, and the pop-top broke off in her hand without opening it. Not to worry—I pulled out the trusty Swiss Army knife on my key ring and chiseled it open, and we settled into our great escape.

The next morning, I was dashing to a tennis match. My key ring is actually a bracelet, with all the keys dangling off it. It was on my right arm, and as I flounced into my car, that arm slammed onto the console between the two front seats, and I felt a sharp stabbing pain. The knife that I had gingerly put away in the darkness of that matinee the day before had sprung and stabbed me in the wrist. Blood was spraying like a faucet all over my newish Prius. I tried to apply pressure to contain the explosion, but I am not a very hearty soul. It is noteworthy here to remember that earlier that year, I had cut the tip of my thumb off while using the bolt cutters on our houseboat-kitchen-remodel project, and that alone had caused me to faint. Helpfully, that was pretty much all I could think about: *I am going to faint and bleed out here in the parking lot!*

I was able to claw my way into my purse with my left hand squeezing my right wrist and hit the last dialed number, which happened to be my sister, who lived a couple miles away. Her husband, Jim, answered the phone and, hearing my distress, told me to call 911. I was not thinking too clearly and deathly afraid that I didn't have another phone call in me, so I begged Mere to just come and run me to the ER. She always helps me be brave. She heroically arrived within minutes, in her pajamas, and got me to the hospital. The vascular surgeon, who was only there one day a week, was miraculously there that morning. He took one look at me, bumped all those carpal tunnel patients in the crowded waiting room, and had me in surgery immediately.

I was loopy when I woke up to find him at my side telling me things went well, and I would soon be fine. I asked him if all his patients fell in love with him, and he shot back, "Have you looked at my face?" It was a great face. I told him I was supposed to play in an important Seniors National Championship in Palm Springs in six weeks. He said, "I don't think I can recommend that." My darling husband had rushed to my side looking pale and a little jealous of my flirtation with my surgeon. In my drugged-out stupor, I told him I needed him to try to do some triage on our car, which was marinating in my blood out there in the parking lot.

Nothing quite like a near-death experience to make one marvel at all the moving pieces that had to be orchestrated from above to allow klutzy moi to survive another day. It was extra-fun for me to email the doctor seven weeks later to tell him he was such a fine surgeon that we went out there and won that tournament.

These are some of my favorite stories, the sacrament-of-the-moment kind, that so far have made up my life, this work in progress. If anything were to happen to me, it would be a shame for these memories to vanish without a trace. Let them be a gift someday to my children and anyone else who wants to listen in. For now, I hope we can just hang on tight to the pieces of heaven we can find here on planet Earth.

# Epilogue

*For there is always light, if we can only be brave enough to see it, if we can only be brave enough to be it.*
—Amanda Gorman

Many of us feel a nostalgic longing for simpler, unplugged times—indeed, the "Make America Great Again" movement captured the imaginations of millions. But going backward and making a mockery of our freedom and our basic human rights has never been the better choice. This is a cruel time for women and not the world I can hand over to my children in good conscience. Regardless of what the conspiracy theorists and propagandists believe, truth still matters, and we *can* handle the truth! We must remember: The only way evil will prosper is for good men and women to do nothing.

I am haunted by the memory of a neon sign that glowed above our table as I had dinner with my friend Amy at a lovely riverside restaurant in Berlin last year: *Capitalism Kills.* Something about that historic city, which bore witness to the terrifying, lingering specter of the Nazi era, taunts me to *pay attention* to the lessons of history in this increasingly materialistic world gone mad.

When I travel abroad, people often ask, "What is going on in your country?" and I cannot explain how we ended up in a science fiction/horror movie in which a fanatical, banner-waving Christian political action committee has worked tirelessly to elect the polar opposite of what Jesus Christ stood for. And yet . . . God is still in charge, allowing us the free will to squander every good and perfect gift we have been given, reminding me not to take the hate-bait that is swirling around, causing me to question everything. All my life God has been faithful to take the low points and weave them into something good. My job is to keep the faith and be ready for any divine appointment he sends my way. I am determined not to be a hypocrite, to take a thorough moral inventory and never give up on hope and grace and truth and love. These are the elemental things that we have a prayer of controlling when the going gets tough.

Episcopal Bishop Mariann Edgar Budde's 2025 inauguration prayer spoke the plainest of truths in calling for dignity and respect and compassion and mercy for all, especially those who are afraid of what the future holds. There is an evolving culture of contempt threatening to undermine every founding value of our country: liberty and justice for *all*, and separation of church and state. A house divided cannot stand.

Rise up, warriors! Reject the lies and radiate your truth. Let your light trump the darkness. Be of good courage. Black lives matter. Women's lives matter. Our children's lives matter. Immigrants' lives matter. May these stories help you feel a little less nuts, laugh a bit, cry a bit, and rededicate yourself to the noble effort of loving one another as if your life depends on it. I am certain that it does.

> *Therefore, we do not lose heart. Though outwardly we are wasting away, yet inwardly we are being renewed day by day. For our light and momentary troubles are achieving for us an eternal glory that far outweighs them all. So we fix our eyes not on what is seen, but on what is unseen. For what is seen is temporary, but what is unseen is eternal.*
>
> —2 Corinthians 4:16–18

# Acknowledgments

Heartfelt thanks to my friend and agent, Amy Rennert, for believing in me, encouraging me, and sharing countless adventures; to Anne Lamott, whose writing is a constant inspiration, who pointed me to our fantastic church and dared me to find an agent—and I only had to look across the tennis court! Huge thanks to Pastor Floyd Thompkins of Saint Andrew Presbyterian Church, Marin City, who lights up my world every week. Oceans of gratitude to Angie Alban for her early reading and editing and encouragement. GrateFULL to my book club mates of twenty years for reading this when it was literally just a journal; to my mom and dad, grandparents, in-laws, and the countless lost loved ones who have spoken so much beauty into my life over the years; to my friend Yaker Kawoh, a brilliant warrior woman who writes and paints and feeds the unhoused and gets more done than any ten people. I am so lucky to have a brilliant posse of friends and family whose lives keep writing these stories—ones that make me slow down and try to preserve every perfect little moment for posterity. Eternal thanks are due to my husband, who shows me daily how to articulate little goals and marvel at what happens from there. I am richly blessed to have all these precious folks to share this lifetime. When I published that article in our local newspaper in honor of Mother's Day, I was literally blown away by the outpouring of encouragement in response to it, much of it from people I didn't think even liked me. I feel a huge debt of gratitude to each one of you who gave me the courage to come out of the closet with my writing.

# About the Author

Liz Krakow is easily mortified and prefers to wear her invisibility cloak most of the time. She writes to try to make sense of life and because it is cheap therapy. She is not now, nor will she ever be, a grown-up.  She never intended these words for publication, but her hot hubby—that is how he has programmed himself into her phone so now it's a well-rehearsed fact—had a bike accident that left him with way too much time on his hands, and he needed a project. She considers the fact that he finally fell in love with her one of her life's greatest achievements. Thanks go to him, Rog III, Lucy, Meredith, Andrew, and her extended family of friends who inspired these stories and taught her everything she ever wanted to know about love.

Liz lives happily ever after on a houseboat in northern California, which rocks her like a cradle daily and has robbed her of all ambition. Names and facts have been tweaked to protect privacy, but these stories really happened.